HEINEMANN POETRY BOOKSHELF

Shakespeare's

Sonnets

Edited by Adrian Raymond

Series Editor: Andrew Whittle
Series Consultant: Virginia Graham

D1584694

Heineman Educational,
a division of Heinemann Publishers (Oxford) Ltd
Halley Court, Jordan Hill, Oxford OX2 8EJ

OXFORD LONDON EDINBURGH
MADRID ATHENS BOLOGNA PARIS
MELBOURNE SYDNEY AUCKLAND SINGAPORE TOKYO
IBADAN NAIROBI HARARE GABORONE PORTSMOUTH NH (USA)

Shakespeare's Sonnets first published in Poetry Bookshelf 1963.
This edition first published 1995.
The publishers and Series Editor are indebted to James Reeves for his work as
Founding Editor of the original Poetry Bookshelf series.

10 9 8 7 6 5 4 3 2 1
99 98 97 96 95

A catalogue record for this book is available from the British Library on request.
ISBN 0 435 150790

Cover design by The Point

Text design by Roger Davies

Typeset by Books Unlimited (Nottm)

Printed by Clays Ltd, St Ives plc

C O N T E N T S

INTRODUCTION

Shakespeare is perhaps the world's most celebrated playwright. As most of his plays are written in verse he may also be regarded as the world's greatest poet. Shakespeare was composing poetry before he became known as a dramatist and his first published work, *Venus and Adonis* was published in 1593.

Shakespeare was born in 1564, early in the reign of Elizabeth I. Unlike many literary figures of his time, he was not university educated but his natural gift soon ensured that he was recognized by his contemporaries and, to a great extent, celebrated in his own lifetime.

The Sonnets

Sonnet writing was extremely fashionable during the 1590s. Shakespeare uses the conventions and form of the sonnet sequence, but he also does much more than that: he often uses the traditional images of love poetry to explore a range of complex emotions and ideas.

Many sonnet sequences of the 1590s were written to a cold-hearted and often inaccessible young woman. Shakespeare's sequence is very different because the first 126 sonnets are addressed to a young man and the remaining sonnets are addressed to a woman with whom the poet has a passionate and tempestuous relationship.

Notes, Critical Approaches and Activities

In this new edition of *Shakespeare's Sonnets*, you will find glossary notes on the pages opposite the poems to help you with unfamiliar words. These pages also include brief summaries and questions to help you think about the poems and develop your own personal responses.

The section *Critical Approaches* introduces you to a variety of ways to approach the study of the sonnets. The Activities help you to put the approaches into practice and develop a range of responses to the poems.

The advice from a chief examiner and essay questions help you to prepare for examinations.

This edition of the text

The Sonnets were published in 1609 by Thomas Thorpe, in the form of a book made from sheets of paper folded into four, known as a Quarto. This edition follows the order of the sonnets in the Thorpe Quarto.

The original spelling has been modernized in this edition to help you to read the sonnets easily.

TO.THE.ONLIE.BEGETTER.OF.
THESE.INSVING.SONNETS.
Mr.W.H. ALL.HAPPINESSE.
AND.THAT.ETERNITIE.
PROMISED.
BY.
OVR.EVER-LIVING.POET.
WISHETH.
THE.WELL-WISHING.
ADVENTVRER.IN.
SETTING.
FORTH.

T.T.

All the poems clearly addressed to a young man are among the first 126 sonnets. In the first 17 sonnets the poet urges his handsome young friend to marry.

1   *increase* – children (with overtones of the continuance of life).
2   *That* – so that.
2   *rose* – in the Quarto edition 'rose' is picked out in italics and with a capital letter. The rose is a romantic symbol in medieval literature and the image places the sonnets in the tradition of courtly love poetry. Some critics have seen it as a clue to the identity of Shakespeare's young man, as 'rose' could be a **pun** (see page 182) on Henry Wriothesley (pronounced 'Rosely') – the Earl of Southampton – but this is far from certain!
5   *contracted* – legally contracted or engaged.
10 *herald* – a herald had the job of announcing the arrival of an important person, or bearing messages for them.
10 *gaudy* – showy
11 An allusion to the canker worm, which eats away the buds of flowers from within and destroys them before they can blossom.
12 *churl* – 1) country bumpkin; 2) brute; 3) miser.
12 *niggarding* – miserliness.

What does the poet mean by 'fairest creatures'?

Why do you think the poet calls the Spring 'gaudy'?

1   *forty* – a common Elizabethan (biblical) synonym for many.
3   *livery* – outward appearance: also uniform, worn by servants.
5–6 *lies, treasure* – both allude to burial in the cold winter ground.
8   *thriftless* – profitless.
11   *sum my count* – total up my account.
12   *succession* – right of inheritance.

How does this sonnet continue the theme and imagery of the first?

In what way is the mood or atmosphere different?

1

From fairest creatures we desire increase,
That thereby beauty's rose might never die,
But as the riper should by time decease,
His tender heir might bear his memory;
5 But thou, contracted to thine own bright eyes,
Feed'st thy light's flame with self-substantial fuel,
Making a famine where abundance lies,
Thyself thy foe, to thy sweet self too cruel.
Thou that art now the world's fresh ornament
10 And only herald to the gaudy spring
Within thine own bud buriest thy content
And, tender churl, mak'st waste in niggarding.
　　Pity the world, or else this glutton be,
　　To eat the world's due, by the grave and thee.

2

When forty winters shall besiege thy brow
And dig deep trenches in thy beauty's field,
Thy youth's proud livery, so gazed on now,
Will be a tattered weed, of small worth held.
5 Then being asked where all thy beauty lies,
Where all the treasure of thy lusty days,
To say within thine own deep-sunken eyes
Were an all-eating shame and thriftless praise.
How much more praise deserv'd thy beauty's use
10 If thou couldst answer 'This fair child of mine
Shall sum my count and make my old excuse,'
Proving his beauty by succession thine.
　　This were to be new made when thou art old,
　　And see thy blood warm when thou feel'st it cold.

1&9 *glass* – mirror, also the window of line 11.

3 *fresh repair* – youthfulness.

5 *uneared* – unploughed, i.e., not producing fruit.
6 *husbandry* – agricultural duties, also sexual responsibilities as a husband.
7 *fond* – foolish and, in this case, self-loving.

13 *golden time* – an allusion to the (mythical) Golden Age of peace and prosperity.

In lines 4–6 what is Shakespeare hinting at?

Is Shakespeare suggesting a way in which we can achieve immortality?

---

1 *unthrifty* – wasteful, unprofitable.
4 *frank* – generous.
5 *beauteous niggard* – beautiful miser.
6 *largess* – generous gift. A word from medieval chivalry.
7 *usurer* – one who lends money at a rate of interest (usury). Although now the basis of Western economic systems, usury was a sin and a crime against the Church before the Reformation (1525 in England). Later, in Shakespeare's time, and up until 1754, usury was illegal if the interest rate charged was higher than specified by law. 'Use' carried a **pun** (see page 182) about sexual activity.
9 *traffic* – business.
12 *audit* – balance sheet, account or final reckoning.
13 *unused* – not invested for profit.
14 *executor* – person who looks after the assets of a dead person's will.

Where in Sonnet 1 does Shakespeare use a similar juxtaposition of charm and miserliness?

3

Look in thy glass, and tell the face thou viewest
Now is the time that face should form another,
Whose fresh repair if now thou not renewest,
Thou dost beguile the world, unbless some mother.
5   For where is she so fair whose uneared womb
Disdains the tillage of thy husbandry?
Or who is he so fond will be the tomb
Of his self-love, to stop posterity?
Thou art thy mother's glass, and she in thee
10 Calls back the lovely April of her prime;
So thou through windows of thine age shalt see,
Despite of wrinkles, this thy golden time.
     But if thou live remembered not to be,
     Die single, and thine image dies with thee.

4

Unthrifty loveliness, why dost thou spend
Upon thyself thy beauty's legacy?
Nature's bequest gives nothing, but doth lend,
And being frank she lends to those are free.
5   Then, beauteous niggard, why dost thou abuse
The bounteous largess given thee to give?
Profitless usurer, why dost thou use
So great a sum of sums yet canst not live?
For having traffic with thyself alone,
10 Thou of thyself thy sweet self dost deceive.
Then how when nature calls thee to be gone,
What acceptable audit canst thou leave?
     Thy unused beauty must be tombed with thee,
     Which, usèd, lives th'executor to be.

1   *frame* – make.
2   *gaze* – object gazed at.
3   *play the tyrants to* – cruelly oppress.
4   *unfair* – (verb) to make ugly.
4   *fairly* – 1) in loveliness 2) completely.
6   *confounds* – defeats, destroys.
7   *lusty* – full of life.

9   *summer's distillation* – the essence of summer, here as in perfume, a liquefied chemical essence held in a glass jar (line 10).

14   *substance* – quality, being; in this case, their scent.

What is the effect of time in this sonnet? (See Time, page 169.)

1   *Then let not...* – the argument continues from Sonnet 5.
1   *ragged* – rough.
3   *vial* – phial or test tube, into which goes the essence, distillation or scent of a flower.
4   *self-killed* – dies naturally with the flower.
5   *usury* – (see 4.7).
6   *happies* – (verb) to bless or make happy.

10   *refigured* – remade; 'figure' can be mathematical or a representation.

How do Sonnets 5 and 6 use the image of perfume?

5

Those hours that with gentle work did frame
The lovely gaze where every eye doth dwell
Will play the tyrants to the very same,
And that unfair which fairly doth excel;
5 For never-resting time leads summer on
To hideous winter and confounds him there,
Sap checked with frost and lusty leaves quite gone,
Beauty o'er-snowed and bareness everwhere:
Then, were not summer's distillation left
10 A liquid prisoner pent in walls of glass,
Beauty's effect with beauty were bereft,
Nor it nor no remembrance that it was.
  But flowers distilled, though they with winter meet,
  Lose but their show; their substance still lives sweet.

6

Then let not winter's ragged hand deface
In thee thy summer ere thou be distilled.
Make sweet some vial, treasure thou some place
With beauty's treasure ere it be self-killed.
5 That use is not forbidden usury
Which happies those that pay the willing loan:
That's for thyself to breed another thee,
Or ten times happier, be it ten for one;
Ten times thyself were happier than thou art,
10 If ten of thine ten times refigured thee.
Then what could death do if thou shouldst depart,
Leaving thee living in posterity?
  Be not self-willed, for thou art much too fair
  To be death's conquest and make worms thine heir.

1   *orient* – the east, where the sun rises.
2   *under* eye – every eye in the world (i.e. every person under the sun).

5   *steep-up* – precipitous.
6   At midday the sun resembles a youth who has grown middle-aged.

9   *car* – chariot, of Phoebus, or Helios, the Sun God in Greek myth, who rides a flaming chariot across the sky each day.
11 *'fore* – before, previously.
14 *get* – beget, to father.

What pun (see page 182) is revealed in the last line of the sonnet?

---

1   *Music to hear* – the poet addresses the Young Man as one whose voice is music to him. Yet the Young Man listens to music sadly.
3   *annoy* – harm, also 'ennui' – boredom.
3–4 The Young Man seems to listen avidly to music yet is made sad or bored by doing so. These lines suggest sadness or melancholy.
5   *concord* – harmony.
7   *chide* – scold.
7   *confounds* – defeats, nullifies.
8   *singleness* – bachelorhood; also one line of a tune (as opposed to many in harmony).
8   *parts* – sexuality, ability to father children, also 'role', with a **pun** (see page 182) on acting; acting the parts of husband and father.
9   *Mark* – take note.
9–10 The lute also has a single top-string, out of harmony with the others. This string represents the Young Man.
11 *sire* – father.

How might the top string of a lute represent the Young Man?

How has Shakespeare created a paradox by comparing the Young Man to music?

7

Lo, in the orient when the gracious light
Lifts up his burning head, each under eye
Doth homage to his new-appearing sight,
Serving with looks his sacred majesty,
5 And having climbed the steep-up heavenly hill,
Resembling strong youth in his middle age,
Yet mortal looks adore his beauty still,
Attending on his golden pilgrimage.
But when from highmost pitch, with weary car,
10 Like feeble age he reeleth from the day,
The eyes, 'fore duteous, now converted are
From his low tract, and look another way.
    So thou, thyself outgoing in thy noon,
    Unlooked on diest unless thou get a son.

8

Music to hear, why hear'st thou music sadly?
Sweets with sweets war not, joy delights in joy.
Why lovest thou that which thou receivest not gladly,
Or else receiv'st with pleasure thine annoy?
5 If the true concord of well tunèd sounds
By unions married, do offend thine ear,
They do but sweetly chide thee, who confounds
In singleness the parts that thou shouldst bear.
Mark how one string, sweet husband to another,
10 Strikes each in each by mutual ordering,
Resembling sire and child and happy mother,
Who all in one one pleasing note do sing;
    Whose speechless song, being many, seeming one,
    Sings this to thee: 'Thou single wilt prove none.'

1–2   The poet suggests the Young Man might be afraid of marriage because his death would make a grieving widow of his wife.

2   *consum'st* – 1) absorb, occupy; 2) destroy.

3   *issueless* – childless.

3   *hap* – happen.

4   *makeless* – matchless, without a mate or husband.

5   *still* – always, forever.

6   *form* – image or picture/statue, reproduction.

7   *private* – individual.

9   *unthrift* – 'big spender'.

9   *spend* – carries a sexual **pun** (see page 182).

12   *unused, user* – both carry the overtone that the 'use' of beauty means sex.

How can the Young Man, sowing his seed, cause his beauty to 'shift...his place'?

How is the image of the 'unthrift' linked with imagery in Sonnets 2, 4 and 6?

---

2   *unprovident* – here, uncaring.

6   *stick'st not* – do not hesitate.

7   *beauteous roof* – body, the house of the soul, the 'self'. Possibly an aristocratic house.

8   *repair* – maintain. Here it means for posterity, like a monument or church.

10   *hate* – self-hatred.

10   *fairer lodged* – more welcome to live in him.

Does this poem suggest that the Young Man is wealthy or aristocratic?

9

Is it for fear to wet a widow's eye
That thou consum'st thyself in single life?
Ah! If thou issueless shalt hap to die,
The world will wail thee, like a makeless wife;
5 The world will be thy widow, and still weep
That thou no form of thee hast left behind,
When every private widow well may keep
By children's eyes her husband's shape in mind.
Look what an unthrift in the world doth spend
10 Shifts but his place, for still the world enjoys it;
But beauty's wastes hath in the world an end,
And kept unused, the user so destroys it.
    No love toward others in that bosom sits
    That on himself such murd'rous shame commits.

10

For shame deny that thou bear'st love to any,
Who for thyself art so unprovident.
Grant, if thou wilt, thou art beloved of many,
But that thou none lov'st is most evident;
5 For thou art so possessed with murderous hate
That 'gainst thyself thou stick'st not to conspire,
Seeking that beauteous roof to ruinate
Which to repair should be thy chief desire.
O, change thy thought, that I might change thy mind!
10 Shall hate be fairer lodged than gentle love?
Be, as thy presence is, gracious and kind,
Or to thyself at least kind-hearted prove.
    Make thee another self, for love of me,
    That beauty still may live in thine or thee.

1–2 If you had a child, as each year passes it would grow at the same rate at which you will decline into old age.

3 *fresh blood* – new life.

3 *youngly* – in your youth.

3 *bestow'st* – give.

8 The world would die in one lifetime.

13 *seal* – image carved in metal, used to show a document to be genuine by printing the author's mark in a soft substance like wax which has been dripped on to the document.

14 *copy* – publishing term for the words of an author, in the abstract, not simply the printed words on the page. If the words are not reprinted, when the original book wears out or is destroyed, the author's words will be forgotten.

How does nature recreate the same image over and over again?

How is the word 'copy' used as a pun?

---

1 *tells* – 'counts' the minutes.

2 *brave* – beautiful, making a show.

4 *sable* – dark brown, from the fur of the animal of that name.

6 *erst* – previously, as in 'erstwhile'.

6 *canopy* – shade.

7 *girded up* – tied up.

8 *bier* – a wooden table, handled like a stretcher for carrying a corpse, but here used to carry the harvest of wheat sheaves home.

9 Therefore I wonder about your beauty.

13 *time's scythe* – the scythe carried by Death in medieval iconography.

14 *breed* – breeding.

14 *to brave him* – to thwart him.

How does the final line alter the tone of the poem?

11

As fast as thou shalt wane, so fast thou grow'st
In one of thine from that which thou departest;
And that fresh blood which youngly thou bestow'st
Thou mayst call thine when thou from youth convertest.
5 Herein lives wisdom, beauty and increase;
Without this, folly, age and cold decay.
If all were minded so, the times should cease,
And threescore year would make the world away.
Let those whom nature hath not made for store,
10 Harsh, featureless, and rude, barrenly perish.
Look, whom she best endowed she gave the more,
Which bounteous gift thou shouldst in bounty cherish.
    She carved thee for her seal, and meant thereby
    Thou shouldst print more, not let that copy die.

12

When I do count the clock that tells the time,
And see the brave day sunk in hideous night;
When I behold the violet past prime,
And sable curls ensilvered o'er with white;
5 When lofty trees I see barren of leaves,
Which erst from heat did canopy the herd,
And summer's green all girded up in sheaves
Borne on the bier with white and bristly beard,
Then of thy beauty do I question make
10 That thou among the wastes of time must go,
Since sweets and beauties do themselves forsake,
And die as fast as they see others grow;
    And nothing 'gainst time's scythe can make defence
    Save breed to brave him when he takes thee hence.

1–2　You have control over your self (or soul) for no longer than the time during which you are alive, here on earth.

3　*Against* – in the event of, anticipating.

5　*in lease* – physical beauty is only loaned or hired out.

6　*determination* – a legal term for the termination of an estate, meaning the whole property of an individual. Usually applied when an estate is being wound up following the owner's death.

8　*form* – (see 9.6).

9　*house* – develops the estate **metaphor** (see page 181) by using a word which can mean either a building or a family e.g. the 'House of Pembroke'.

10　*husbandry* – thrift, care with money, to preserve the estate intact. Here, also punned (see page 183) to suggest 'becoming a husband'.

12　*barren* – sterile or unfruitful.

> **What does Shakespeare suggest the Young Man's son should inherit?**

2　*astronomy* – what we would think of as 'astrology', that is, predicting the future from the motion of the planets.

4　*dearths* – droughts, shortages.

5　Nor can I predict events accurately to the minute.

8　By often predicting what I find in the stars – the heavens.

10　*read such art* – predict this story.

13　*prognosticate* – foretell.

14　*doom* – destiny.

> **What idea is Shakespeare exploring in this sonnet?**

13

O that you were yourself! But, love, you are
No longer yours than you yourself here live.
Against this coming end you should prepare,
And your sweet semblance to some other give.
5 So should that beauty which you hold in lease
Find no determination; then you were
Yourself again after your self's decease,
When your sweet issue your sweet form should bear.
Who lets so fair a house fall to decay,
10 Which husbandry in honour might uphold
Against the stormy gusts of winter's day,
And barren rage of death's eternal cold?
    O, none but unthrifts, dear my love, you know.
    You had a father; let your son say so.

14

Not from the stars do I my judgement pluck,
And yet methinks I have astronomy;
But not to tell of good or evil luck,
Of plagues, of dearths, or seasons' quality.
5 Nor can I fortune to brief minutes tell,
Pointing to each his thunder, rain, and wind,
Or say with princes if it shall go well
By oft predict that I in heaven find:
But from thine eyes my knowledge I derive
10 And, constant stars, in them I read such art
As truth and beauty shall together thrive,
If from thyself to store thou wouldst convert
    Or else of thee this I prognosticate:
    Thy end is truth's and beauty's doom and date.

4   The stars influence the 'world stage' like the playwright influences his characters.

8   *wear* – wear out.
8   *brave state* – proud beauty.
9   *conceit* – **irony** (see page 180).
9   *inconstant stay* – finite, or fixed-term life.
11 *debateth with decay* – 1) discusses with; 2) argues with; 3) fights with.

14 *engraft* – when gardeners graft a cutting on to a rooted plant, they combine the best qualities of each plant into a new one, called a 'hybrid'. Shakespeare uses it as a **synonym** (see page 182) for rebirth.

What is Shakespeare hinting at in line 11? Does Time discuss with, argue with or fight with decay? Are they enemies?

---

4   *means* – measures, appropriate actions.
5   *happy hours* – blessed time, i.e. blessed with his life still standing before him. The phrase has been debased in modern times by publicans!
6   *maiden gardens* – virgins' wombs.
8   Much more lifelike than a painting of you.
10 *pencil...pen* – a pencil was a very fine paintbrush, used to paint miniature portraits – the 'painted counterfeit'. A pen would only have been used for writing.
11–12 The poet says that a man's soul cannot be transferred to another man by any form of art: the Young Man cannot live in another man's eyes, or head. The only way his essence, or 'self,' can be transferred is into his own children.

How would 'maiden gardens yet unset' in line 6 bear fruit?

If this is a poem about sex, is the tone formal, informal, or vulgar?

15

When I consider every thing that grows
Holds in perfection but a little moment,
That this huge stage presenteth naught but shows
Whereon the stars in secret influence comment;
5   When I perceive that men as plants increase,
Cheerèd and checked even by the selfsame sky;
Vaunt in their youthful sap, at height decrease,
And wear their brave state out of memory:
Then the conceit of this inconstant stay
10   Sets you most rich in youth before my sight,
Where wasteful time debateth with decay
To change your day of youth to sullied night;
        And all in war with time for love of you,
        As he takes from you, I engraft you new.

16

But wherefore do not you a mightier way
Make war upon this bloody tyrant, time,
And fortify yourself in your decay
With means more blessèd than my barren rhyme?
5   Now stand you on the top of happy hours,
And many maiden gardens yet unset
With virtuous wish would bear your living flowers
Much liker than your painted counterfeit.
So should the lines of life that life repair
10   Which this time's pencil, or my pupil pen
Neither inward worth nor outward fair
Can make you live yourself in eyes of men.
        To give away yourself keeps yourself still,
        And you must live drawn by your own sweet skill.

Sonnet 17 is viewed by some critics as the last in the sequence urging the Young Man to marry.

2   *deserts* – deserved praises.

8   *ne'er* – never.

11 *rage* – madness associated with delirium, plague, rabies.
12 *stretchèd metre* – forced metre, or false-sounding words added simply to fit the poetic rhythm.

In lines 3–4, why does the poet think that his verse is like a 'tomb'?

2   *temperate* – mild, as in the weather and as in kindness, or warmth.
3   *winds* – always pronounced to rhyme with 'mind' in Shakespeare's time.
3   *May* – the month which produces tender early growth.
4   *lease* – allotted time-span. Legal term (see 13.5).
7   *fair* – beauty.
7   *sometime* – at some point in time.
8   *chance* – bad luck, which shortens or changes the natural course of things.
10 *lose* – also to release.
10 *ow'st* – 1) to own; 2) to owe.
11 *brag* – death cannot boast of entire possession of him if his memory lives on.

How can Shakespeare have the confidence (line 14) that this poem will last as long as ever men live?

Does Shakespeare, in line 10, think that beauty is the possession of a young person, or only borrowed?

17

Who will believe my verse in time to come
If it were filled with your most high deserts?-
Though yet, heaven knows, it is but as a tomb
Which hides your life, and shows not half your parts.
5 If I could write the beauty of your eyes
And in fresh numbers number all your graces,
The age to come would say 'This poet lies;
Such heavenly touches ne'er touched earthly faces.'
So should my papers, yellowed with their age,
10 Be scorned, like old men of less truth than tongue,
And your true rights be termed a poet's rage
And stretchèd metre of an antique song.
    But were some child of yours alive that time,
    You should live twice: in it, and in my rhyme.

18

Shall I compare thee to a summer's day?
Thou art more lovely and more temperate.
Rough winds do shake the darling buds of May,
And summer's lease hath all too short a date.
5 Sometime too hot the eye of heaven shines,
And often is his gold complexion dimmed,
And every fair from fair sometime declines.
By chance, or nature's changing course untrimmed;
But thy eternal summer shall not fade
10 Nor lose possession of that fair thou ow'st,
Nor shall death brag thou wander'st in his shade
When in eternal lines to time thou grow'st,
    So long as men can breathe or eyes can see,
    So long lives this, and this gives life to thee.

Some critics see Sonnet 19 (rather than Sonnet 17) as the last in the sequence persuading the Young Friend to marry and have children in order to defy time. In this sonnet Shakespeare addresses time itself and claims his verse will allow his 'love' to triumph over time and remain young.

4 *phoenix* – one phoenix was said to be alive at any time; it died in its own flames and the new bird appeared from its ashes.

8 *heinous* – terrible, horrific.

10 *antique* – long-lived, and carries the suggestion of antic, or manic, mad, like Hamlet's 'antic disposition'.

13 *despite* – in spite of ill-fortune (see 36.6).

Do you see this poem as a natural end to the first sequence of sonnets?

The sonnet is full of shifting ambiguities. Some critics have viewed Sonnet 20 as proof that the poet's love for the Friend was of a homosexual nature: others believe Sonnet 20 implies that the relationship between the poet and the Friend was *not* sexual.

2 *master-mistress* – an **oxymoron** (see page 181) for the mixed-up gender which is the subject of the poem.

3–4 A heart which was gentle but not fickle or flirtatious.

5 *rolling* – roving, in a lustful way.

6 *Gilding* – he makes those on whom he gazes feel as precious and beautiful as gold.

7 A man in shade, all shades of men in his controlling.

7 *controlling* – in his control or 'in awe of him'.

8 *steals* – thieves (verb); possibly 'steels' or strengthens, linking back to 'Gilding' in line 6.

8 *amazeth* – overwhelms, reduces to jelly.

8 *eyes...soul* – possibly a bawdy **pun** (see page 182) – eye: female genital, soul: male genital, linked to 'master-mistress' in line 2.

9 *for a woman* – to be a woman.

11 *nature* – Mother Nature, traditionally a female goddess.

12 *to my purpose nothing* – of no interest to me. Also 'no thing' – the sexual organ.

13 *pricked thee out* – 1) gave you a prick; 2) marked your name in the register.

14 *love's use* – the male organ (slang).

19

Devouring time, blunt thou the lion's paws,
And make the earth devour her own sweet brood;
Pluck the keen teeth from the fierce tiger's jaws,
And burn the long-lived phoenix in her blood;
5   Make glad and sorry seasons as thou fleet'st,
And do whate'er thou wilt swift-footed time,
To the wide world and all her fading sweets.
But I forbid thee one most heinous crime:
O, carve not with thy hours my love's fair brow,
10 Nor draw no lines there with thine antique pen.
Him in thy course untainted do allow
For beauty's pattern to succeeding men.
     Yet do thy worst, old time; despite thy wrong
     My love shall in my verse ever live young.

20

A woman's face with nature's own hand painted
Hast thou the master-mistress of my passion;
A woman's gentle heart but not acquainted
With shifting change as is false women's fashion;
5   An eye more bright than theirs, less false in rolling,
Gilding the object whereupon it gazeth;
A man in hue, all hues in his controlling,
Which steals men's eyes and women's souls amazeth.
And for a woman wert thou first created,
10 Till nature as she wrought thee fell a-doting,
And by addition me of thee defeated
By adding one thing to my purpose nothing.
     But since she pricked thee out for women's pleasure,
     Mine be thy love and thy love's use their treasure.

1 *muse* – used here as 'a poet'. The sonnet becomes an attack on over-extravagant sonnets in general.

2 *stirred* – inspired.

3 *ornament* – a small, decorative flourish, used in both poetry and in music.

4 compares every kind of beauty (fair) with the beauty of his subject. The subject would seem to be male.

4 *rehearse* – request, compare.

5 *couplement* – comparison, association.

7 *rondure* – the arch of the sky; sometimes thought to be a parody of the style of George Chapman.

12 *gold candles* – stars.

13 *hearsay* – there is a suggestion of 'like the sound of their own voices' in this line.

What is Shakespeare saying about the difference between his verse and verse 'Stirred by a painted beauty'?

---

1 *glass* – mirror.

2 *of one date* – of the same age, i.e. 'thou art youthful'.

3 *furrows* – wrinkles.

4 *expiate* – make amends for.

5 *seemly raiment* – appropriate garment.

11 *chary* – carefully.

In lines 13–14, what does the poet fear will happen to their love after his death?

21

So is it not with me as with that muse
Stirred by a painted beauty to his verse,
Who heaven itself for ornament doth use,
And every fair with his fair doth rehearse,
5   Making a couplement of proud compare
With sun and moon, with earth and sea's rich gems,
With April's first-born flowers, and all things rare
That heaven's air in this huge rondure hems.
O let me, true in love, but truly write,
10 And then believe me my love is as fair
As any mother's child, though not so bright
As those gold candles fixed in heaven's air.
    Let them say more that like of hearsay well;
    I will not praise, that purpose not to sell.

22

My glass shall not persuade me I am old
So long as youth and thou are of one date;
But when in thee time's furrows I behold,
Then look I death my days should expiate.
5   For all that beauty that doth cover thee
Is but the seemly raiment of my heart,
Which in thy breast doth live, as thine in me,
How can I then be elder than thou art?
O therefore, love, be of thyself so wary,
10 As I, not for myself, but for thee will,
Bearing thy heart, which I will keep so chary,
As tender nurse her babe from faring ill.
    Presume not on thy heart when mine is slain:
    Thou gav'st me thine not to give back again.

1 *unperfect actor* – player who has not properly learned his lines.

2 *is put beside his part* – forgets his lines.

3 *replete* – full to overflowing.

6 *rite* – a ceremony, usually religious. Here, 'love's' may mean the god of love or sexual intercourse.

8 *o'er charged* – overcharged, overwhelmed.

8 *burthen* – burden, weight, also a tune or melody.

10 *dumb presagers* – 'silent prophecies' (see **oxymoron**, page 181).

11 *recompense* – return of love offered by pleading words.

14 *To hear with eyes* – reading the words.

Looking at lines 13-14, which is the poet's most important sense – hearing or sight?

In this sonnet the poet imagines himself looking into the eyes of the Young Man.

1 *play'd* – acted the part.

1 *steeled* – engraved.

2 *table* – notebook.

4 *perspective* – in Elizabethan painting, the 'perspective' meant more than a simple three-dimensional appearance to a flat picture. Elizabethan artists played a variety of tricks with perspective, making images which were indecipherable unless looked upon in a certain way, or from a particular angle, like modern 'magic eye' pictures. The most famous is Holbein's *The Ambassadors* where the distorted shape in the foreground appears as a skull only when viewed by someone mounting a staircase. Another technique was the perspective frame, which was a viewing glass which corrected the distorted image to make it clear. The **metaphor** (see page 181) which Shakespeare plays with here is that the true beauty of his subject can only be seen in a certain way, and that way is through his own, poet's eyes.

6 *true image* – a picture is only a resemblance, not a true image. A picture is also self-contained in its own world, defined by the frame around it.

Why is the theatre similar to the metaphor in line 6?

What is your interpretation of this sonnet? Do you think it is a successful poem? Why (not)?

What are the 'good turns' of line 9?

23

As an unperfect actor on the stage
Who with his fear is put besides his part,
Or some fierce thing replete with too much rage
Whose strength's abundance weakens his own heart,
5 So I, for fear of trust, forget to say
The perfect ceremony of love's rite,
And in mine own love's strength seem to decay
O'ercharged with burthen of mine own love's might.
O let my books be then the eloquence
10 And dumb presagers of my speaking breast,
Who plead for love, and look for recompense,
More than that tongue that more hath more expressed.
    O learn to read what silent love hath writ;
    To hear with eyes belongs to love's fine wit.

24

Mine eye hath play'd the painter and hath steeled
Thy beauty's form in table of my heart.
My body is the frame wherein 'tis held,
And perspective it is best painter's art.
5 For through the painter must you see his skill
To find where your true image pictured lies,
Which in my bosom's shop is hanging still,
That hath his windows glazèd with thine eyes.
Now see what good turns eyes for eyes have done,
10 Mine eyes have drawn thy shape, and thine for me
Are windows to my breast, where-through the sun
Delights to peep, to gaze therein on thee.
    Yet eyes this cunning want to grace their art:
    They draw but what they see, know not the heart.

1 *stars* – astrological reference, familiar to modern readers of horoscopes, that the stars incline to good/bad fortune. Maybe the subject of the poem is a rich patron, a 'star' who has it in his power to give or remove favour from the poet.

4 *unlooked-for* – unexpected.

5 *their* – the favourites'.

6 *as the marigold* – like a marigold opens to the sun.

9 *painful warrior* – soldier wounded or suffering pain.

Why is a marigold in line 6 an appropriate image?

What do you think 'famousèd for worth' means in line 9?

Why is the poet so sure of his love in lines 13–14, and why is he more certain of it than of fame?

---

1 *vassalage* – feudal obedience, service.

3 *embassage* – embassy, diplomatic message.

4 *not to show my wit* – Shakespeare refutes the charge he makes against the flattering marigolds in Sonnet 25.

7 *conceit* – opinion; that the poem will give rise to an idea in the subject's mind more interesting or clever than the literary devices used in the poem itself. (See **conceit** page 179.)

8 *all naked* – the subject's mind.

11 *apparel* – clothes.

14 *prove* – test.

To what does the poet compare his mind in line 8?

25

Let those who are in favour with their stars
Of public honour and proud titles boast,
Whilst I, whom fortune of such triumph bars
Unlooked-for joy in that I honour most.
5   Great princes' favourites their fair leaves spread,
But as the marigold at the sun's eye,
And in themselves their pride lies burièd,
For at a frown they in their glory die.
The painful warrior famousèd for worth,
10   After a thousand victories once foiled
Is from the book of honour razèd quite,
And all the rest forgot for which he toiled.
      Then happy I, that love and am beloved
      Where I may not remove, nor be removed.

26

Lord of my love, to whom in vassalage
Thy merit hath my duty strongly knit,
To thee I send this written embassage
To witness duty, not to show my wit;
5   Duty so great, which wit so poor as mine
May make seem bare, in wanting words to show it:
But that I hope some good conceit of thine
In thy soules thought, all naked, will bestow it:
Till whatsoever star that guides my moving
10   Points on me graciously with fair aspect,
And puts apparel on my tattered loving
To show me worthy of thy sweet respect.
      Then may I dare to boast how I do love thee;
      Till then, not show my head where thou mayst prove me.

2   *travel* – Quarto has 'travail' which can also mean 'work'.

5   *from far where I abide* – far from where I live.
6   *Intend* – set out in thought.

10 *shadow* – image, picture. This recalls the theme of image against reality
    which was such a part of Sonnet 24.

How is the imagination like a journey?

2   *debarr'd* – deprived of.
3   *day's oppression* – daily toil or labour.

6   *shake hands* – agree.

8   *How far I toil* – how far he is away.
11 *swart* – dark, or black. Similar to modern word 'swarthy'.
12 *twire* – peep out.
12 *gildst the even* – the Quarto spelling, 'guil'st th'eaven', allows a range of
    punning (see page 182) in this line.
13–14 The poet counts each passing day and night, watching it add to the length of
    their separation. There may also be a hint of spring as the working day
    grows longer each day.

What does the night remind the poet of in line 8?

27

Weary with toil, I haste me to my bed,
The dear repose for limbs with travel tired;
But then begins a journey in my head
To work my mind, when body's work's expired;
5 For then my thoughts, from far where I abide,
Intend a zealous pilgrimage to thee,
And keep my drooping eyelids open wide,
Looking on darkness which the blind do see:
Save that my soul's imaginary sight
10 Presents thy shadow to my sightless view,
Which like a jewel hung in ghastly night
Makes black night beauteous, and her old face new.
    Lo thus by day my limbs, by night my mind,
    For thee, and for myself, no quiet find.

28

How can I then return in happy plight
That am debarred the benefit of rest,
When day's oppression is not eased by night
But day by night and night by day oppressed,
5 And each, though enemies to either's reign,
Do in consent shake hands to torture me,
The one by toil, the other to complain
How far I toil, still farther off from thee?
I tell the day to please him thou art bright,
10 And do'st him grace when clouds do blot the heaven;
So flatter I the swart-complexioned night
When sparkling stars twire not thou guildst the even.
    But day doth daily draw my sorrows longer
    And night doth nightly make grief's length seem stronger.

3 *bootless* – pointless, unanswered.

6 This line suggests no one individual in particular.
7 *scope* – range of talents.
8 So unhappy that my usual favourite pastimes become a burden to me.
10 *Haply* – by chance or 'by good fortune, I happen to...'.
11 *heaven's gate* – the lark flies high above the fields at dawn and sings a beautiful song of praise to daybreak.

14 I would not be persuaded to change places with a king.

---

1 *sessions* – the time when a court of law is in operation.
2 His thoughts are like witnesses in a court of law.
3 I sigh for things I can remember but can no longer have.
4 *new wail* – mourn afresh.
4 *my dear time's waste* – the passing of my life.
5 *drown an eye* – cry bitterly.
6 *dateless* – endless.
7 *a fresh* – afresh, again.
7 *love's long-since cancelled woe* – the pain of old loves, which has been erased by new loves.
8 *th'expense* – the spending of; the fact that the vanished sights are experiences which, once spent, can never be relived.
11 *tell o'er* – count over, count up.

> **What effect does the wordplay in line 12 achieve?**

29

When in disgrace with fortune and men's eyes,
I all alone beweep my outcast state,
And trouble deaf heaven with my bootless cries,
And look upon myself and curse my fate,
5   Wishing me like to one more rich in hope,
Featured like him, like him with friends possessed,
Desiring this man's art and that man's scope,
With what I most enjoy contented least:
Yet in these thoughts myself almost despising,
10 Haply I think on thee, and then my state,
Like to the lark at break of day arising
From sullen earth, sings hymns at heaven's gate,
    For thy sweet love remembered such wealth brings
    That then I scorn to change my state with kings'.

30

When to the sessions of sweet silent thought
I summon up remembrance of things past,
I sigh the lack of many a thing I sought,
And with old woes new wail my dear time's waste.
5   Then can I drown a eye unused to flow
For precious friends hid in death's dateless night,
And weep a fresh love's long-since-cancelled woe,
And moan th'expense of many a vanished sight.
Then can I grieve at grievances foregone,
10 And heavily from woe to woe tell o'er
The sad account of fore-bemoanèd moan,
Which I new pay as if not paid before.
    But if the while I think on thee, dear friend,
    All losses are restored, and sorrows end.

1   *endeared* – made precious, endowed.

5   *obsequious* – respectful, as in sadness at a funeral ceremony.

6   *religious* – pure, reverent.

6   *stol'n from* – taken from, prompted from.

7   *interest* – that which is due.

8   *But* – 'simply as'.

8   *removed* – separated, at a distance.

11   *their parts of me* – the character of the mature poet has taken on attributes of previous lovers, some now dead. He projects all these qualities on to his new beloved.

12   *due of many* – these qualities are a debt owed to many different people from whom they were borrowed.

14   You are the sum of all of their finest qualities and all of me, put together.

This poem has very strong masculine endings and makes extensive use of the extra syllable on 'èd' past tenses. What effect does this have on the rhythm of the poem? Does it also affect the tone?

---

1   *day* – life.

2   *churl* – brute (see 1.12).

3   *by fortune...resurvey* – happen to read.

5   See how they have survived time, whereas the mortal poet has been 'bettered' or killed by it.

8   *height* – fame.

8   *happier* – more fortunate.

9   *vouchsafe me* – promise me.

9   *but* – only, simply.

10   *my friend's* – the poet's.

10   *grown with this growing age* – moved with the fashion.

11   *dearer birth* – created more valuable poetry.

12   *equipage* – military equipment.

13   *prove* – new poets are more advanced or fashionable.

What fear does the poet show in this sonnet, especially in line 13?

31

Thy bosom is endearèd with all hearts
Which I by lacking have supposèd dead,
And there reigns love and all love's loving parts,
And all those friends which I thought burièd.
5   How many a holy and obsequious tear
Hath dear religious love stol'n from mine eye
As interest of the dead, which now appear
But things removed that hidden in thee lie!
Thou art the grave where buried love doth live,
10   Hung with the trophies of my lovers gone,
Who all their parts of me to thee did give:
That due of many, now is thine alone.
      Their images I loved I view in thee,
      And thou, all they, hast all the all of me.

32

If thou survive my well-contented day,
When that churl death my bones with dust shall cover,
And shalt by fortune once more resurvey
These poor rude lines of thy deceasèd lover:
5   Compare them with the bett'ring of the time,
And though they be outstripped by every pen,
Reserve them for thy love, not for their rhyme
Exceeded by the height of happier men.
O then vouchsafe me but this loving thought:
10   'Had my friend's Muse grown with this growing age,
A dearer birth than this his love had brought
To march in ranks of better equipage;
      But since he died, and poets better prove,
      Theirs for their style I'll read, his for his love.'

Sonnets 33–35 speak of a rift in the relationship between the poet and the Friend.

In Sonnet 34 the Friend is associated with the 'sun'. Some critics see the reference to 'this disgrace' as evidence that Shakespeare had a physical relationship with 'the Friend'. Alternatively 'disgrace' may refer to the fact that the Friend has abandoned the poet.

1   *Full many* – very many.

2   *Flatter* – beautify. Flattery literally means 'beautify', unlike the modern word which often implies insincerity.

4   *alchemy* – the art of turning base metal into gold, the predecessor of modern chemistry.

5   *basest* – the clouds remind the poet of base metals, such as lead, as compared with the precious metal of the golden sun. Shakespeare also uses 'base' as meaning 'not of noble worth'.

12   *region cloud* – over-arching cloud, high in the heavens.

14   *Suns of the world* – great men, or mortals (punning on 'sons').

14   *stain* – darken; be discoloured or corrupted, sin.

14   *staineth* – is darkened, covered, or discoloured by clouds. Also 'abstains' or goes away.

2   *travel* – also work, implying a laborious journey.

3   *base* – not of noble worth.

4   *brav'ry* – splendour, beauty.

7   *salve* – ointment, cure.

8   Heals the wound but does not remove the scar, which is the evidence.

9   *physic* – medicine.

14   *ransom* – pay for, pay the debt (biblical), Christ being the ransom to pay the debt caused by the sins of the world.

Sonnet 34 continues the theme and imagery of Sonnet 33. The Friend appears to have returned. Is this enough to win the poet's forgiveness?

33

Full many a glorious morning have I seen
Flatter the mountain tops with sovereign eye,
Kissing with golden face the meadows green,
Gilding pale streams with heavenly alchemy;
5 Anon permit the basest clouds to ride
With ugly rack on his celestial face,
And from the forlorn world his visage hide
Stealing unseen to west with this disgrace.
Even so my sun one early morn did shine
10 With all triumphant splendour on my brow;
But out alas, he was but one hour mine;
The region cloud hath masked him from me now.
    Yet him for this my love no whit disdaineth;
    Suns of the world may stain when heaven's sun staineth.

34

Why didst thou promise such a beauteous day,
And make me travel forth without my cloak,
To let base clouds o'ertake me in my way,
Hiding thy brav'ry in their rotten smoke.
5 'Tis not enough that through the cloud thou break
To dry the rain on my storm-beaten face,
For no man well of such a salve can speak
That heals the would and cures not the disgrace.
Nor can thy shame give physic to my grief;
10 Though thou repent, yet I have still the loss.
Th'offender's sorrow lends but weak relief
To him that bears the strong offence's cross.
    Ah but those tears are pearl which thy love sheds
    And they are rich, and ransom all ill deeds.

3   *stain* – darken.

4   *canker* – The canker worm grew in the buds of plants such as the rose and destroyed the bud from within.

7   By corrupting myself I provide an ointment for your injury.

8   To cancel out the sin, the excuse must be bigger than the sin itself.

9   *sensual fault...sense* – I bring intellectual reasoning and justification ('sense') to excuse your 'sensual fault'.

10 *adverse party...advocate* – the opponent in a court case is also the lawyer for the defence (meaning the poet is both the prosecution and defence).

13 *accessory* – a helper of the lawbreaker in his or her crime.

In Sonnets 33 and 34 Shakespeare appears to blame the Friend for the rift in their relationship and in this sonnet he blames the Friend in the first line ('that which thou hast done'). How does this sonnet show that Shakespeare also blames himself?

What do you think the 'sweet thief' is? It could be a) the Friend's sensuality; b) Shakespeare's own sensual nature; c) a woman (see Sonnets 40–42).

---

1   *twain* – two, apart. Shakespeare chooses the word to emphasize that he and his beloved will be two separate beings.

3   *blots* – usually taken to mean some form of disgrace or dishonour, as in Sonnet 29, perhaps.

6   *separable spite* – an ill-fortune which separates them.

10 *bewailèd guilt* – either a disgrace, as the 'blots' in line 3 to be made public (bewailed), or a private shame to be regretted (bewailed).

11 *honour* – acknowledge, recognize, possibly support as a patron.

12 Without dishonouring yourself or losing social standing.

12 *report* – reputation.

Why does the poet say he and the Friend may not see each other? What do you think the poet means in the last two lines?

35

No more be grieved at that which thou hast done:
Roses have thorns, and silver fountains mud.
Clouds and eclipses stain both moon and sun,
And loathsome canker lives in sweetest bud.
5   All men make faults, and even I in this,
Authorizing thy trespass with compare,
Myself corrupting salving thy amiss,
Excusing thy sins more than my sins are:
For to thy sensual fault I bring in sense–
10   Thy adverse party is thy advocate–
And 'gainst my self a lawful plea commence,
Such civil war is in my love and hate
     That I an accessory needs must be,
     To that sweet thief which sourly robs from me.

36

Let me confess that we two must be twain
Although our undivided loves are one;
So shall those blots that do with me remain
Without thy help by me be borne alone.
5   In our two loves there is but one respect,
Though in our lives a separable spite
Which though it alter not love's sole effect,
Yet doth it steal sweet hours from love's delight.
I may not evermore acknowledge thee
10   Lest my bewailèd guilt should do thee shame,
Nor thou with public kindness honour me
Unless thou take that honour from thy name.
     But do not so, I love thee in such sort
     As, thou being mine, mine is thy good report.

8   *engrafted* – see 15.14.

8   *store* – the store of good qualities he sees embodied in the young man.

10 *shadow* – idea; also life, existence, soul. A **metaphor** (see page 181) for
    the transience of life, usually comparing the human condition to that of
    a character portrayed on stage. An 'idea' made flesh, or made real, just
    as the player makes ideas, the invented people of the playwright come
    alive as real flesh and blood.

10 *substance* – reality, the player becomes the substance of the playwright's
    thoughts.

14 *happy* – blessed. This is important because 'happy' then contrasts with the
    misfortunes referred to in lines 1–4.

What do you think line 3 means?

2   *breathe* – breath is here 'the life-force' (as in 'the breath of God') and it
    is the young man's life-force which 'breathes life into' the poem.

3   *argument* – story-line or subject of a poem.

6   *worthy perusal* – worth studying.

7   *to thee* – about you.

8   *light* – life (see Sonnet 37).

9   *tenth muse* – Greek mythology has nine muses, goddesses who inspire
    human beings with creativty.

9   *rhymers* – (from Old French verb) poets, writers of rhyme.

9   *invocate* – invoke.

12 *Eternal numbers* – infinite numbers. A phrase coined to mean numbers
    which can last 'beyond date' or beyond defined time. Numbers also
    implies 'verses', such as sonnets which conform to strict numerical
    patterns.

37

As a decrepit father takes delight
To see his active child do deeds of youth,
So I, made lame by fortune's dearest spite
Take all my comfort of thy worth and truth;
5 For whether beauty, birth, or wealth or wit,
Or any of these all, or all, or more,
Entitled in their parts do crownèd sit,
I make my love engrafted to this store.
So then I am not lame, poor, nor despised,
10 Whilst that this shadow doth such substance give
That I in thy abundance am sufficed,
And by a part of all thy glory live.
    Look what is best, that best I wish in thee;
    This wish I have, then ten times happy me.

38

How can my muse want subject to invent
While thou dost breathe that pour'st into my verse
Thine own sweet argument, too excellent
For every vulgar paper to rehearse?
5 O, give thyself the thanks if ought in me
Worthy perusal stand against thy sight;
For who's so dumb that cannot write to thee,
When thou thyself dost give invention light?
Be thou the tenth muse, ten times more in worth
10 Than those old nine which rhymers invocate,
And he that calls on thee, let him bring forth
Eternal numbers to outlive long date.
    If my slight muse do please these curious days,
    The pain be mine, but thine shall be the praise.

1 *manners* – appropriately, in respect of the social difference between poet and subject.

6 *lose* – also release, let loose.

8 *That due* – that which is due to.

9 *thou prove* – Shakespeare often seems to have difficulty distinguishing between the real young man and the idea of him (see 37.10 and 38.8). In this line the poet fails to distinguish between the separation and the man, calling the man, and not the separation, a torment.

10 *sour leisure* – similar to line 9 where it is the fact of the young man being elsewhere at his leisure which is sour, not the leisure itself. This is like a rejected lover who questions whether to blame the other person or fate.

Compare this sonnet with Sonnet 36.

In Sonnets 40–42 it seems the poet reluctantly accepts that his Friend has become his mistress's lover.

5 *for my love* – 1) as a substitute for my affection (love); 2) out of affection for me (i.e. you love what I love because you love me); 3) to win more of my affection (by taking what the woman enjoys).

5 *thou my love receives* – you entertain my mistress.

6 *For my love thou usest* – 1) I cannot blame you for having sex with my mistress; 2) I cannot blame you because you do it for love of me.

10 *steal thee* – steal for yourself.

10 *poverty* – everything I have amounts to poverty, including a faithless mistress.

11 *gentle thief* – an **oxymoron** (see page 181) contrasting the subject's noble status with his actions.

13 *Lascivious grace* – **oxymoron** (see page 181) contrasting lust with grace.

There are many different interpretations of lines 5–6. Which best suits your reading? Why? Do you think the poet intended all readings, thereby undermining his forgiveness of the Friend?

39

O, how thy worth with manners may I sing,
When thou art all the better part of me?
What can mine own praise to mine own self bring,
And what is't but mine own when I praise thee?
5   Even for this, let us divided live,
And our dear love lose name of single one,
That by this separation I may give
That due to thee which thou deserv'st alone.
O absence what a torment wouldst thou prove.
10   Were it not thy sour leisure gave sweet leave
To entertain the time with thoughts of love,
Which time and thoughts so sweetly dost deceive,
    And that thou teachest how to make one twain
    By praising him here who doth hence remain!

40

Take all my loves, my love, yea take them all,
What hast thou then more than thou hadst before?
No love, my love, that thou mayst true love call–
All mine was thine before thou hadst this more.
5   Then if for my love thou my love receivest,
I cannot blame thee, for my love thou usest;
But yet be blam'd, if thou this self deceivest
By wilful taste of what thyself refusest.
I do forgive thy robb'ry gentle thief
10   Although thou steal thee all my poverty;
And yet love knows it is a greater grief
To bear love's wrong, than hate's known injury.
    Lascivious grace, in whom all ill well shows,
    Kill me with spites yet we must not be foes.

1   *pretty* – 1) petty; 2) wanton, sexual; 3) appealing.

2   *sometime* – 1) sometimes; 2) for some time.

3–4   His beauty and his youth befit the 'pretty wrongs' or suggest temptations which probably arise when the poet is away.

5   *Gentle* – noble, kind (see 40.11).

6   *assailed* – tried for, attempted.

8   *he* – sometimes changed to 'she'.

9   *my seat forbear* – the poet hopes the young man might vacate his position (seat) respecting the mistress by chiding (controlling the effect of) his youth and beauty.

11   *riot even there* – wanton, immoral behaviour even with the poet's mistress. Is nothing sacred?

12   *forced to* – necessarily.

12   *troth* – trust, truth, promise – the troth 'plighted' in a marriage service.

14   *false* – there could be a betrayal of friendship as much as there could be a betrayal of love implied by this line.

> *Why does the poet feel the Friend's relationship with the Woman is not entirely the Friend's fault?*

---

3   *of my wailing chief* – the main cause of my distress.

9   *lose* – also to release.

8   *Suff'ring* – allowing.

8   *approve her* – try her out, appreciate her.

11   *both twain* – both together, both of them.

12   *for my sake* – for love of me.

12   *cross* – difficulty, problem; (biblical) 'we all have our cross to bear'.

14   *Sweet flattery* – tempting gloss, interpretation.

> *In line 11 the poet feels that the Friend and his mistress both gain from their relationship while he loses 'both twain'. Yet in the final couplet he states that, since he and the Friend are 'one', his mistress loves 'but me alone'. How convincing do you find these last two lines?*

41

Those pretty wrongs that liberty commits,
When I am sometime absent from thy heart
Thy beauty, and thy years full well befits,
For still temptation follows where thou art.
5 Gentle thou art and therefore to be won;
Beauteous thou art, therefore to be assailed;
And when a woman woos, what woman's son,
Will sourly leave her till he have prevailed?
Ay me, but yet thou might'st my seat forbear,
10 And chide thy beauty and thy straying youth,
Who lead thee in their riot even there
Where thou art forced to break a two-fold troth
    Hers, by thy beauty tempting her to thee,
    Thine by thy beauty being false to me.

42

That thou hast her, it is not all my grief,
And yet it may be said I loved her dearly;
That she hath thee is of my wailing chief,
A loss in love that touches me more nearly.
5 Loving offenders, thus I will excuse ye:
Thou dost love her, because thou know'st I love her,
And for my sake even so doth she abuse me,
Suff'ring my friend for my sake to approve her.
If I lose thee, my loss is my love's gain,
10 And losing her, my friend hath found that loss:
Both find each other, and I lose both twain,
And both for my sake lay on me this cross,
    But here's the joy: my friend and I are one.
    Sweet flattery! Then she loves but me alone.

1 *When most I wink* – when my eyes are tightest shut.

2 *unrespected* – unnoticed.

4 *darkly bright* – **oxymoron** (see page 181), describing how his eyes being shut are dark and yet see bright visions in dreams.

5 *shadow shadows* – idea, spirit, memory. The first 'shadow' means the *thought* of the young man, the remembrance of him. This gives rise to a shadow in the dreaming mind. A shadow of the mind is like an actor playing upon the stage of a dream, filling the darkness of the room with light and texture and colouring out the shadows of the night, to banish them (see Sonnet 37).

6 *form* – shape.

6 *form happy show* – bless him by making a show, a play in his mind.

8 *shade* – 1) an essence of him; 2) a variation of 'shadow'; 3) the influence of him.

9 How much finer is a real person than the memory of them?

10 *the living day* – 1) daylight; 2) in real life.

12 *fair imperfect shade* – beautiful but unreal.

---

1 *dull* – inert, solid; also uninteresting, uninspiring.
substance – material being, essence (see Sonnets 53 and 37).

5 *No matter then* – 1) if this were so, it would not matter that...; 2) if flesh were thought it would not be matter.

9 *thought...thought* – the understanding (thought) that I cannot travel to you as fast as thought ('I am not thought') is 'devastating' ('kills me').

11 *so much* – such a thing.

11 *of earth and water wrought* – made of two of the so-called four elements, earth, air, fire and water. Earth and water are duller and 'lower' than fire and air.

12 *time's leisure* – the length of time that Time chooses to take; possibly short for 'time's pleasure'.

14 *badges* – indications, signs.

14 *either's woe* – the woe of each element. The tears represent earth by being heavy and water by being wet.

43

When most I wink, then do my eyes best see,
For all the day they view things unrespected,
But when I sleep, in dreams they look on thee,
And, darkly bright, are bright in dark directed.
5   Then thou, whose shadow shadows doth make bright,
How would thy shadow's form form happy show,
To the clear day with thy much clearer light,
When to unseeing eyes thy shade shines so!
How would, I say, mine eyes be blessèd made,
10 By looking on thee in the living day,
When in dead night thy fair imperfect shade
Through heavy sleep on sightless eyes doth stay!
     All days are nights to see till I see thee,
     And nights bright days when dreams do show thee me.

44

If the dull substance of my flesh were thought,
Injurious distance should not stop my way;
For then despite of space I would be brought,
From limits far remote, where thou dost stay.
5   No matter then although my foot did stand
Upon the farthest earth removed from thee;
For nimble thought can jump both sea and land
As soon as think the place where he would be.
But ah, thought kills me that I am not thought,
10 To leap large lengths of miles when thou art gone,
But that so much of earth and water wrought,
I must attend time's leisure with my moan.
     Receiving naught by elements so slow
     But heavy tears, badges of either's woe.

1 *air...fire* – medieval science believed that matter was composed of four elements which became four corresponding 'humours' in the human being: blood, melancholy (or black bile), choler and phlegm. In the body, the proportions of the humours which make up a particular individual were believed to determine personality. A person with a great deal of black bile would be habitually miserable, whereas a phlegmatic person would have an insipid, watery personality. Here, 'Slight air' becomes thought and 'purging fire' becomes pure desire, or passion.

5 *quicker* – more lively, lighter.

6 *embassy* – message.

8 *Sinks down to death* – 1) drowns in water; 2) becomes listless and apathetic, phlegmatic.

9 *composition* – balance of the humours. Illness was held to arise from an imbalance of the humours; if the humours were equally balanced the person would be perfect.

9 *recured* – put back together, re-balanced, cured.

10 *swift messengers* – the humours, as a letter.

> *In line 14, why does the poet grow sad when he returns the messengers?*

Sonnets 46 and 47 explore a conflict between the eye (*desire* for the Friend) and the heart (his *love*). Conflict between the eye and heart is conventional in Renaissance poetry.

2 *conquest* – spoils of war.

4 *freedom* – privileges.

5 *in him dost lie* – he carries love like treasure in a box.

6 *closet* – a jewellery box, a cupboard or a private chamber.

6 *empanellèd* – legal term for a sworn-in jury.

10 *quest* – short for 'inquest'.

12 *clear* – like crystal, implying that the eye must be pure.

12 *moiety* – half.

> *At what point are military terms replaced by legal ones?*

> *It is unusual to rhyme on the same word. Why has Shakespeare done so here?*

45

The other two, slight air, and purging fire,
Are both with thee, wherever I abide;
The first my thought, the other my desire,
These present-absent with swift motion slide;
5   For when these quicker elements are gone
In tender embassy of love to thee,
My life, being made of four, with two alone,
Sinks down to death, oppressed with melancholy.
Until life's composition be recured,
10   By those swift messengers returned from thee,
Who even but now come back again assured
Of thy fair health, recounting it to me.
     This told, I joy; but then no longer glad,
     I send them back again and straight grow sad.

46

Mine eye and heart are at a mortal war
How to divide the conquest of thy sight.
Mine eye my heart thy picture's sight would bar,
My heart mine eye the freedom of that right.
5   My heart doth plead that thou in him dost lie,
A closet never pierced with crystal eyes;
But the defendant doth that plea deny,
And says in him thy fair appearance lies.
To 'cide this title is empanelled
10   A quest of thoughts, all tenants to the heart,
And by their verdict is determinèd
The clear eye's moiety, and the dear heart's part.
     As thus: mine eye's due is thy outward part,
     And my heart's right, thine inward love of heart.

1   *league* – an agreement, a pact. This idea follows directly on from Sonnet 46.

6   *bids* – invites. The eye plays the role of host to the heart here.

9   *love* – like a memory in his mind, his love is ever-present in his heart, though he may not always be conscious of it.

10 *Thyself away* – you, when you are away.

11 *no* – Quarto gives 'nor', sometimes amended to 'not'.

11 *than* – can be read either as 'then', for 'therefore', or as 'than', for 'you are no further away than thoughts'.

12 *still* – 1) always; 2) calm.

What is the league between eyes and heart?

Sonnets 48 and 49 explore the shifting nature of the Friend.

1   *careful* – full of care.

2   *trifle* – trivial thing.

2   *truest bars* – the sense is taken from storing valuables in a vault, barred against thieves. The **metaphor** (see page 181) stands for his rib-cage, his ribs being the bars protecting his heart. Thus 'truest' means 'most honest' being his own.

3   *to my use* – exclusive to me.

5   *jewels trifles* – his beloved regards the poet's dearest thoughts as mere trifles.

8   *Art left* – remain.

10 *save* – except. The line means that the beloved is locked in his heart where he feels love – a place where the beloved could not physically be.

11 *closure* – enclosure.

12 *at pleasure* – 1) you can come and go as you please; 2) you are free to go and take pleasure.

14 *deare* – 1) adored; 2) hard to bear, grievous.

Why does truth prove thievish (line 14)?

Do you think the poet is suggesting the Friend will be passively taken from him or that the Friend might actively leave him?

47

Betwixt mine eye and heart a league is took,
And each doth good turns now unto the other.
When that mine eye is famished for a look,
Or heart in love with sighs himself doth smother,
5   With my love's picture then my eye doth feast,
And to the painted banquet bids my heart.
Another time mine eye is my heart's guest
And in his thoughts of love doth share a part.
So either by thy picture or my love,
10   Thyself away are present still with me;
For thou no farther than my thoughts canst move,
And I am still with them, and they with thee;
    Or if they sleep, thy picture in my sight
    Awakes my heart, to heart's and eye's delight.

48

How careful was I when I took my way
Each trifle under truest bars to thrust,
That to my use it might unusèd stay
From hands of falsehood, in sure wards of trust.
5   But thou, to whom my jewels trifles are,
Most worthy comfort, now my greatest grief,
Thou best of dearest and mine only care
Art left the prey of every vulgar thief.
Thee have I not locked up in any chest,
10   Save where thou art not, though I feel thou art–
Within the gentle closure of my breast,
From whence at pleasure thou mayst come and part;
    And even thence thou wilt be stol'n I fear,
    For truth proves thievish for a prize so dear.

1   *Against that time* – in preparation for the moment.

2   *defects* – second syllable stressed to rhyme with 'respects'.

3   *When as* – whereas.

3   *cast* – throw, tot up (accounts).

3   *utmost sum* – the final, total sum of love that the beloved will pay.

4   *Called* – brought or called to account.

4   *audit* – examination of an account book, meaning the account cannot be used.

4   *advised respects* – well-considered, sensible thoughts.

5   *strangely pass* – pass by as a stranger would, without acknowledgement.

8   *settled gravity* – 1) shall find reasons to pass by with composed dignity (gravitas); 2) love shall end because you have found out grave, indisputable reasons for doing so; 3) 'love' reaches a comfortable old age.

9   *ensconce* – from Old Scots word for a small fortress, in which the poet seeks to barricade himself.

10 *desert* – 1) deserving; 2) deserted. Both meanings are present.

11 The poet is like a witness who swears (raises his hand) to testify against himself, or like a soldier who threatens himself with his own hand.

14 The poet can find no reason why the Friend should love him. However, the poet is also condemning the Friend here, suggesting that no reason can be given why *anyone* should be loved.

In Sonnets 48 and 49 the poet appears to be defending the Friend. Yet he is also attacking the Friend's changing nature. Identify the ambiguous lines and phrases. How does the poet feel about the Friend at this point?

What is there in this sonnet to suggest the subject was socially superior to Shakespeare?

3   *that ease ... that repose* – that particular ease/repose

6   *weight* – the Quarto spelling 'waite' is close to 'wait' and therefore introduces the idea that time can also be measured by the passing miles.

Which line in this sonnet could be put in quotation marks?

What is the 'anger' in line 9 which makes the poet dig the bloody spurs into his 'beast'? Does he feel remorse for this in line 12?

49

Against that time–if ever that time come–
When I shall see thee frown on my defects,
When as thy love hath cast his utmost sum,
Called to that audit by advised respects;
5   Against that time when thou shalt strangely pass
And scarcely greet me with that sun, thine eye,
When love converted from the thing it was
Shall reasons find of settled gravity.
Against that time I do ensconce me here
10   Within the knowledge of mine own desert,
And this my hand against my self uprear
To guard the lawful reasons on thy part.
    To leave me poor thou hast the strength of laws,
    Since why to love I can allege no cause.

50

How heavy do I journey on the way,
When what I seek – my weary travel's end–
Doth teach that ease and that repose to say
'Thus far the miles are measured from my friend.'
5   The beast that bears me, tired with my woe,
Plods dully on, to bear that weight in me,
As if by some instinct the wretch did know
His rider loved not speed, being made from thee.
The bloody spur cannot provoke him on
10   That sometimes anger thrusts into his hide,
Which heavily he answers with a groan
More sharp to me than spurring to his side;
    For that same groan doth put this in my mind:
    My grief lies onward and my joy behind.

1 *my love* – my feeling of love (not 'my beloved').
4 *of posting* – of hurrying.

6 *swift extremity* – extreme speed, explained in line 7.

8 *no motion shall I know* – it will seem as if I am not moving.
9 *Then* – if, because.
11 *This fiery race* – its lineage or course (with an association between desire and the element fire).
12 *love, for love* – 1) love, out of compassion; 2) love, out of desire (see 49.14)
12 *jade* – broken-down old horse.
14 *I'll run* – probably metaphorical (see page 181), meaning his thoughts or his desire will run on ahead.
   leave to go – 1) excuse him from the task; 2) permission to walk rather than to gallop.

Where in the sonnet do we hear the actual excuse mentioned in lines 1, 5 and 12?

4 *seldom* – infrequent.
6 *seldom coming* – spaced far apart.

8 *captain* – chief, most important. Possibly with a hinted overtone of 'captive'.
8 *carcanet* – gold, jewelled necklace.
9 *chest* – treasure chest (see Sonnet 48).
12 *pride* – object of value.
14 *triumph* – rejoice, celebrate.

Why does the poet describe pleasure as a 'fine point'?

51

Thus can my love excuse the slow offence
Of my dull bearer when from thee I speed:
From where thou art why should I haste me thence?
Till I return, of posting is no need.
5   O what excuse will my poor beast then find
When swift extremity can seem but slow?
Then should I spur, though mounted on the wind;
In wingèd speed no motion shall I know.
Then can no horse with my desire keep pace;
10   Therefore desire, of perfect'st love being made,
Shall rein no dull flesh in his fiery race;
But love, for love, thus shall excuse my jade:
    Since from thee going he went wilful-slow,
    Towards thee I'll run and give him leave to go.

52

So am I as the rich whose blessèd key
Can bring him to his sweet up-lockèd treasure,
The which he will not ev'ry hour survey,
For blunting the fine point of seldom pleasure.
5   Therefore are feasts so solemn and so rare
Since, seldom coming in the long year set
Like stones of worth they thinly placèd are,
Or captain jewels in the carcanet.
So is the time that keeps you as my chest,
10   Or as the wardrobe which the robe doth hide,
To make some special instant special blest,
By new unfolding his imprisoned pride.
    Blessèd are you whose worthiness gives scope,
    Being had, to triumph; being lacked, to hope.

1   *substance* – essential nature, being (see also 44.1).

2   *shadows* – unreal beings (perhaps flatterers).

2   *tend* – attend, wait upon you. 'Tend' may also suggest 'incline towards you', i.e. try to be like you'.

3   *one shade* – shadow.

5   *Adonis* – a beautiful youth loved by the Greek goddess of Love, Aphrodite.

5   *counterfeit* – picture.

7   *Helen* – Helen of Troy, the model of female beauty.

7   *set* – 1) are set; 2) sit.

8   *tires* – attire, costume, clothes.

9   *foison* – natural produce, harvest, generosity of nature.

13 *some part* – some partner, someone to compare with you.

14 In constancy you exceed everybody: nobody has such constancy as you.

Many critics have commented that the praise of the Friend in this sonnet is incompatible with the person described in Sonnets 40–42. Others have suggested the sonnet is a piece of direct irony and have interpreted the last line as 'you feel affection for no one and no one admires you for the virtue of constancy'. Do you think this sonnet is ironic?

---

3   *fair* – beautiful.

3   *deem* – consider it to be.

4   *live* – the scent becomes the quintessence of the rose.

5   *canker blooms* – dog rose flowers. Every so often a cultivated rose throws out a dog rose stem, which has a seven leaf pattern and unscented flowers. These stems are usually pruned.

5   *dye* – the Quarto spelling 'die' emphasizes the **puns** death, orgasm: (see page 182).

6   *tincture* – essence, either of colour or scent – here both!

9   *for* – because.

9   *show* – appearance, their only virtue.

10 *unrespected* – unnoticed, their value paid no respect.

10 *distils* – removing the concentrated essence.

10 *truth* – personality, spirit, quintessence.

Compare the theme of this sonnet with Sonnets 15–19.

53

What is your substance, whereof are you made,
That millions of strange shadows on you tend?
Since every one hath, every one, one shade,
And you, but one, can every shadow lend.
5   Describe Adonis and the counterfeit,
Is poorly imitated after you.
On Helen's cheek all art of beauty set,
And you in Grecian tires are painted new.
Speak of the spring and foison of the year:
10   The one doth shadow of your beauty show,
The other as your bounty doth appear,
And you in every blessèd shape we know.
    In all external grace you have some part,
    But you like none, none you, for constant heart.

54

Oh how much more doth beauty beauteous seem
By that sweet ornament which truth doth give!
The rose looks fair, but fairer we it deem
For that sweet odour which doth in it live.
5   The canker blooms have full as deep a dye
As the perfumèd tincture of the roses,
Hang on such thorns, and play as wantonly
When summer's breath their maskèd bud discloses;
But for their virtue only is their show
10   They live unwooed and unrespected fade,
Die to themselves. Sweet roses do not so;
Of their sweet deaths are sweetest odours made:
    And so of you, beauteous and lovely youth,
    When that shall fade, by verse distils your truth.

2   *powerful* – three syllables, asked to do the work of two, give strength to the word.
3   *these contents* – what is written here (accent on second syllable).
6   *broils* – local skirmishes.
6   *work of masonry* – mason's art.
7   *burn* – only the quick fire can burn, not Mars's sword, yet the verb seems to apply to both (see **zeugma**, page 182).
9   *oblivious enmity* – enemy forces working to *cause* your oblivion, or annihilation (utter destruction).
11 *all posterity* – all who live after him.
12 *wear this world out* – survive this world.
12 *ending doom* – final judgement.

The theme of love triumphing over time through the immortality of verse was common in Renaissance literature. Shakespeare's source was probably Golding's translation of the Metamorphoses of Ovid or the Odes of Horace. In these poems, however, it is the poet himself who is immortal. Shakespeare is bestowing immortality on the Friend through his verse.
Which lines do you think contribute most to the resounding note of confidence in this sonnet?

For an extended activity on this sonnet, see page 166.

2   *thy edge* – sword blade.
3   *allayed* – satisfied; held at bay.
6   *wink with fullness* – sleepy after a huge meal.
8   *dullness* – darkness.
10 *contracted new* – newly betrothed lovers.
11 *banks* – water's edge.
12 *return of love* – 1) possibly the ocean (a metaphor for love) returning with the tide; 2) the sail of the beloved's ship returning across the ocean.
12 *blessed* – beautiful.
14 *rare* – valuable.

To what extent do you think this sonnet is about separation and to what extent do you think it is about the renewal of love?

55

Not marble nor the gilded monuments
Of princes shall outlive this powerful rhyme
But you shall shine more bright in these contents
Than unswept stone besmeared with sluttish time.
5 When wasteful war shall statues overturn,
And broils root out the work of masonry,
Nor Mars his sword, nor war's quick fire shall burn
The living record of your memory.
'Gainst death, and all oblivious enmity
10 Shall you pace forth; your praise shall still find room
Even in the eyes of all posterity
That wear this world out to the ending doom.
    So, till the judgement that your self arise,
    You live in this, and dwell in lovers' eyes.

56

Sweet love, renew thy force. Be it not said
Thy edge should blunter be than appetite,
Which but today by feeding is allayed,
Tomorrow sharpened in his former might.
5 So, love, be thou; although today thou fill
Thy hungry eyes even till they wink with fullness,
Tomorrow see again, and do not kill
The spirit of love, with a perpetual dullness.
Let this sad int'rim like the ocean be
10 Which parts the shore where two contracted new,
Come daily to the banks, that when they see
Return of love, more blessed may be the view.
    Or call it winter, which, being full of care,
    Makes summer's welcome, thrice more wished, more rare.

4   *require* – order.

5   *chide the world-without-end hour* – complain about the never-ending time (of your absence). 'World without end' would have been easily recognized as the ending of the Lord's Prayer.

8   *adieu* – French form of 'goodbye', meaning 'God keep you.'

11   *stay* – be still, control myself.

12   *happy* – happy (in modern sense), blessed.

13   *your will* – your desire, **pun** on penis and on 'William' (see page 182).

> *What reasons can you find for the formal 'You/your' form of address rather than the intimacy of 'thou/thy'?*

> *Do you think the tone of this sonnet is much bitterer than in previous sonnets in the Quarto sequence? Why(not)?*

1–2   May the God who first made me your slave forbid that I should curb your pleasure even in my mind.

2   *pleasure* – like 'will' (see 57.13), 'pleasure' has sexual overtones.

3   Ask you to write down the details of what you do at what hour.

5   *beck* – beckon, as in 'at your beck and call'.

6   *imprisoned absence* – an **oxymoron** (see page 182) The whole line plays with the conceit that the beloved's absence is a form of imprisonment to the poet.

7   *sufferance* – the ability to suffer it, to endure it.

9   *where you list* – where you like.

9   *charter* – a feudal charter gave a Lord the power to judge cases at law – to pardon or to sentence criminals. Here it suggests the beloved's noble status and his freedom through power.

10   *privilege* – apportion.

14   *pleasure* – decision. In line 2, *pleasure* refers to the Friend's enjoyable pastimes and has sexual overtones. The word carries the same sense here but also has overtones of 'at your (majesty's) pleasure' emphasising the power the Friend has over the poet.

57

Being your slave, what should I do but tend
Upon the hours and times of your desire?
I have no precious time at all to spend,
Nor services to do, till you require;
5 Nor dare I chide the world-without-end hour
Whilst I, my sovereign, watch the clock for you,
Nor think the bitterness of absence sour
When you have bid your servant once adieu.
Nor dare I question with my jealous thought
10 Where you may be, or your affairs suppose,
But like a sad slave stay and think of nought
Save, where you are, how happy you make those.
    So true a fool is love, that in your will,
    Though you do anything he thinks no ill.

58

That god forbid, that made me first your slave,
I should in thought control your times of pleasure,
Or at your hand th'account of hours to crave,
Being your vassal bound to stay your leisure.
5 O let me suffer, being at your beck,
Th'imprisoned absence of your liberty,
And patience, tame to sufferance, bide each check,
Without accusing you of injury.
Be where you list, your charter is so strong,
10 That you your self may privilege your time
To what you will, to you it doth belong,
Yourself to pardon of self-doing crime.
    I am to wait, though waiting so be hell,
    Not blame your pleasure, be it ill or well.

1 *is* – exists already.

2 *beguiled* – tricked.

4 *burden* – pregnancy.

1–4 If there is nothing new, if all that is has been before, how are we tricked into imagining that what we write is original, when the same thing has in fact been said before?

5 *record* – memory on second syllable (stressed).

6 *five hundred courses of the sun* – 600 years ago. The poet uses the 'Great Year' of 120 years to evoke an old astrological belief that 600 years previously, the configuration of sun and stars would have been the same.

8 Since thoughts were first put into writing.

9 *composèd wonder* – praise composed in verse.

9–10 That I might compare that old description with mine.

11 *mended* – improved.

11 *whe'er* – in which respects.

12 *revolution* – whether the latest astrological cycle produces a world identical to the last.

---

5 *Nativity* – birth, but also an astrological term for the precise configuration of stars at the moment of birth.

5 *main* – sea, region.

7 *crooked* – malignant.

8 *confound* – destroy.

9 *transfix* – pierce through

9 *flourish* – 1) blossom, beautiful flower; 2) decoration; 3) wave a weapon.

10 *parallels* – wrinkles.

10 *delves* – digs, ploughs.

11 *rarities of nature's truth* – the finest things in nature.

12 *scythe* – in medieval iconography, Death often carries a scythe which reaps all living things when they die (hence the 'Grim Reaper').

13 *to times* – to aftertimes, to the future.

14 'my' refers to the Friend, 'his' to the Beloved.

Compare the poet's view of time in this sonnet with his view of time in Sonnet 55.

59

If there be nothing new, but that which is
Hath been before, how are our braines beguiled,
Which, labouring for invention, bear amiss
The second burden of a former child!
5   O that record could with a backward look
Even of five hundred courses of the sun,
Show me your image in some antique book
Since mind at first in character was done.
That I might see what the old world could say,
10   To this composèd wonder of your frame;
Whether we are mended, or whe'er better they,
Or whether revolution be the same.
    O, sure I am the wits of former days
    To subjects worse have given admiring praise.

60

Like as the waves make towards the pebbled shore,
So do our minutes hasten to their end,
Each changing place with that which goes before;
In sequent toil all forwards do contend.
5   Nativity, once in the main of light,
Crawls to maturity, wherewith being crowned,
Crookèd eclipses 'gainst his glory fight,
And time that gave, now doth his gift confound.
Time doth transfix the flourish set on youth,
10   And delves the parallels in beauty's brow;
Feeds on the rarities of nature's truth,
And nothing stands but for his scythe to mow.
    And yet to times in hope my verse shall stand,
    Praising thy worth despite his cruel hand.

4   *shadows* – see 37.10 and 43.5.

8   *tenure* – the right of his jealousy to occupy the poet's mind at night.

Is this a sonnet of despair or a sonnet of love, or both? Compare this sonnet with Sonnet 27.

---

  1   *Sin of self-love* – vanity, love of his own identity.
  4   *grounded* – taken root, taken such hold.
  6   *such account* – worth so much.
7–8   *do define As I* – 'do define like this…'
  8   *all worths* – every respect.
  9   *glass* – mirror.
 10   *beated* – beaten, as in 'weather-beaten'.
 10   *tanned* – The effect of the sun on skin was held to be ugly. A tan was regarded as the mark of those who had to work outside to survive and this would indicate a low status. Rich women would not be obliged to spend time outside and therefore remained very pale-skinned.
 14   *age* – old age.
 14   *days* – youth.

The poet begins this sonnet by accusing himself of vanity (self-love). However, in the final couplet he identifies his 'self' with the Friend. How convincing do you find the last couplet as an excuse for the poet's vanity?

61

Is it thy will, thy image should keep open
My heavy eyelids to the weary night?
Dost thou desire my slumbers should be broken
While shadows like to thee do mock my sight?
5 Is it thy spirit that thou send'st from thee
So far from home into my deeds to pry,
To find out shames and idle hours in me,
The scope and tenure of thy jealousy?
O no; thy love, though much, is not so great.
10 It is my love which keeps mine eye awake,
Mine own true love that doth my rest defeat,
To play the watchman ever for thy sake.
    For thee watch I whilst thou dost wake elsewhere,
    From me far off, with others all too near.

62

Sin of self-love possesseth all mine eye,
And all my soul, and all my every part;
And for this sin there is no remedy,
It is so grounded inward in my heart.
5 Me thinks no face so gracious is as mine,
No shape so true, no truth of such account,
And for myself mine own worth do define
As I all other in all worths surmount.
But when my glass shows me myself indeed,
10 Beated and chapped with tanned antiquity,
Mine own self-love quite contrary I read;
Self so self-loving were iniquity.
    'Tis thee, myself, that for myself I praise,
    Painting my age with beauty of thy days.

1   *Against* – in the event of (my love becoming as I am now – see Sonnets 13 and 49).

3   *drained his blood* – as people aged they were thought to have less 'blood' and so became paler.

3   *filled* – also filed with a sense of defiled or disfigured.

5   *steepy* – 1) precipitous, suggestive of a tremendous, steep drop; 2) sharp decline.

8   *Stealing* – two senses – of theft and of stealth.

9   *fortify* – (see 49.9)

14   *green* – young. (In **Love's Labour's Lost** Armado says 'Green indeed is the colour of lovers'. 1.2.83)

---

1   *fell* – fearsome, cruel.

3   *down razed* – ruined, destroyed, razed to the ground.

4   *mortal rage* – corrosion, corruption, fatal disease, possibly with an overtone of madness. (see 17.11)

8   *store* – capital, reserves.

10   *confounded* – destroyed.

14   *lose* – (see 18.10)

13–14   The circle of life where having must also mean losing because time cannot be stopped.

> *The poet talks of gains and losses made by the sea and land in lines 5–8. What is gained and what is lost, and how does this illustrate the poet's meaning?*

63

Against my love shall be as I am now,
With time's injurious hand crushed and o'erworn,
When hours have drained his blood and filled his brow
With lines and wrinkles; when his youthful morn
5 Hath travelled on to age's steepy night,
And all those beauties whereof now he's king
Are vanishing, or vanished out of sight,
Stealing away the treasure of his Spring:
For such a time do I now fortify
10 Against confounding age's cruel knife,
That he shall never cut from memory
My sweet love's beauty, though my lover's life.
    His beauty shall in these black lines be seen,
    And they shall live, and he in them still green.

64

When I have seen by time's fell hand defaced
The rich proud cost of outworn buried age,
When sometime-lofty towers I see down razed,
And brass eternal slave to mortal rage;
5 When I have seen the hungry ocean gain
Advantage on the kingdom of the shore,
And the firm soil win of the wat'ry main,
Increasing store with loss, and loss with store;
When I have seen such interchange of state,
10 Or state itself confounded to decay,
Ruin hath taught me thus to ruminate:
That time will come and take my love away.
    This thought is as a death, which cannot choose
    But weep to have that which it fears to lose.

1 *since* – since there is neither.
   nor – the constructions 'neither...nor' and 'either...or' did not exist in Shakespeare's day. He generally uses the form 'nor...nor' and 'or...or' instead.

2 *But* – can prevent.

3 *rage* – see 64.4.

6 *wrackful siege* – wrecking siege.

10 *time's best jewel from time's chest* – 1) the best jewel from time's chest; 2) the young man is time's best jewel, trying to hide from the coffin – time's chest.

12 *spoil* – 1) ruin; 2) spoils of war.

---

1 *Tired* – fatigued, **pun** (see page 182) on attired.

2 *As* – for example. This begins a list of eleven examples.

2 *desert a beggar born* – merit born into poverty.

3 A poor nobody dressed up in fine robes.

4 *unhappily forsworn* – unfortunately betrayed.

5 *gilded* – gold covering means true worth.

5 *misplaced* – mis-used.

6 *strumpeted* – 1) given over to prostitution; 2) violated; 3) falsely reputed as promiscuous.

7 *wrongfully disgraced* – brought falsely into scandal.

8 *disabled* – four syllables, to rhyme with line 6.

10 *doctor-like* – 1) like a scholar; 2) like a lawyer.

11 *simple truth* – common sense.

12 Good is the prisoner of ill, now its commanding officer (see 52.8).

13 *would I be* – I wish to be.

14 *Save that* – except that.

14 *to die* – if I were to die.

This form is unique in the Quarto. Why is it used?

65

Since brass, nor stone, nor earth, nor boundless sea,
But sad mortality o'ersways their power,
How with this rage shall beauty hold a plea,
Whose action is no stronger than a flower?
5 O how shall summer's honey breath hold out
Against the wrackful siege of battering days,
When rocks impregnable are not so stout,
Nor gates of steel so strong, but time decays?
O fearful meditation! where, alack,
10 Shall time's best jewel from time's chest lie hid,
Or what strong hand can hold his swift foot back,
Or who his spoil of beauty can forbid?
    O none, unless this miracle have might,
    That in black ink my love may still shine bright.

66

Tired with all these, for restful death I cry:
As, to behold desert a beggar born,
And needy nothing trimmed in jollity,
And purest faith unhappily forsworn,
5 And gilded honour shamefully misplaced,
And maiden virtue rudely strumpeted,
And right perfection wrongfully disgraced,
And strength by limping sway disablèd,
And art made tongue-tied by authority,
10 And folly, doctor-like, controlling skill,
And simple truth miscalled simplicity,
And captive good attending captain ill.
    Tired with all these, from these would I be gone,
    Save that to die I leave my love alone.

The reference to the Friend as *he* in this poem marks a crucial stage in Shakespeare's account of the Friend.

1   *wherefore* – why.
1   *infection* – 1) a **metaphor** (see page 181) for sin or corruption; 2) early cosmetics were notoriously toxic.
2   *grace impiety* – 1) bless, condone sinful behaviour; 2) wearing cosmetics may have been regarded as sinful.
3   *That sin* – 1) sinful behaviour; 2) of wearing cosmetics.
3   *by him* – sin runs through him like infected blood.
4   *lace itself* – 1) dress itself up in fine lace clothes; 2) entwine itself.
4   *society* – company.
5   *false painting* – cosmetics, hiding the signs of ageing.
6   *dead seeing* – make-up is not living, but seems real.
6   *living hue* – the colour of a face full of life.
8   *Roses of shadow* – falsely represented youth.
10 *veins* – Quarto has spelling 'vaines' to carry the hint of vanity.
11 *no exchequer now but his* – nature has no treasury other than him because he has no successor in beauty.

What is nature bankrupt of in line 9?

Some critics have interpreted this sonnet as praise of the Friend at the expense of the sickly, corrupted world ('infection') described in Sonnet 66. However, given that the Friend's moral shortcomings are emphasized in earlier sonnets it is also possible to read it as suggesting the Friend's 'nature' is corrupt even though he is beautiful. Try to identify examples to support each reading.

1   *Thus* – the sonnet follows on from Sonnet 67.
2   *died* – Quarto has 'dyed' to allow visual pun (see page 182) on dye.
5   *golden tresses of the dead* – Elizabethan wigs were made from hair of the dead. The idea does not seem to appeal!
6   *sepulchres* – tombs.
8   *gay* – attractive, dressed up.
9   *holy antique hours* – the reverence and dignity of age.
10 *Without all ornament* – without any cosmetic addition.

67

Ah, wherefore with infection should he live
And with his presence grace impiety,
That sin by him advantage should achieve
And lace itself with his society?
5   Why should false painting imitate his cheek,
And steal dead seeing of his living hue?
Why should poor beauty indirectly seek
Roses of shadow, since his rose is true?
Why should he live now nature bankrupt is,
10 Beggared of blood to blush through lively veins,
For she hath no exchequer now but his,
And proud of many, lives upon his gains?
    O, him she stores to show what wealth she had
    In days long since, before these last so bad.

68

Thus is his cheek the map of days outworn,
When beauty lived and died as flowers do now,
Before these bastard signs of fair were borne
Or durst inhabit on a living brow;
5   Before the golden tresses of the dead,
The right of sepulchres, were shorn away
To live a second life on second head,
Ere beauty's dead fleece made another gay.
In him those holy antique hours are seen
10 Without all ornament, itself and true,
Making no summer of another's green,
Robbing no old to dress his beauty new;
    And him as for a map doth nature store,
    To show false art what beauty was of yore.

2 *mend* – improve.

4 *as foes commend* – if an enemy praises, it is worth believing.

9–10 The beauty of thy mind they measure, at a guess, by looking at thy deeds.

11 Then their thoughts become churlish, unpleasant.

12 *flower* – appearance, outward beauty (see Sonnets 60 and 67).

> What are the different meanings of 'soil' in line 14 and what is meant by
> 'thou dost common grow'?

1 *defect* – fault.

2 *mark* – used here to mean target, victim.

3 Beauty is suspected to be artificial (see 68.10) and covering up something less worthy.

4 *A crow* – a common Elizabethan insult meaning ugliness. Shakespeare was referred to as 'an upstart crow' by Robert Greene, a playwright, in an open letter to fellow players.

5 *So thou be good* – if you are good, then...

5 *slander* – personified as the gossip or talk of the town which will bear out his goodness (see **personification** page 182).

6 *being wooed of time* – wooed by time.

9 *the ambush of young days* – being ambushed into temptation by youthful high spirits and young lust.

10 *assailed* – attacked.

13 *some suspect* – some suspicion.

13–14 Fortunately, your bad reputation has masked your beauty a little, otherwise whole kingdoms of hearts would have been broken by now.

> Compare this view of the Friend with the description of the Friend in other
> sonnets.

69

Those parts of thee that the world's eye doth view
Want nothing that the thought of hearts can mend.
All tongues, the voice of souls, give thee that due,
Uttering bare truth, even so as foes commend.
5   Thy outward thus with outward praise is crowned,
But those same tongues that give thee so thine own
In other accents do this praise confound
By seeing farther than the eye hath shown.
They look into the beauty of thy mind,
10 And that in guess they measure by thy deeds.
Then, churls, their thoughts–although their eyes were kind–
To thy fair flower add the rank smell of weeds.
    But why thy odour matcheth not thy show,
    The soil is this: that thou dost common grow.

70

That thou are blamed shall not be thy defect,
For slander's mark was ever yet the fair.
The ornament of beauty is suspect,
A crow that flies in heaven's sweetest air.
5   So thou be good, slander doth but approve
Thy worth the greater, being wooed of time;
For canker vice the sweetest buds doth love,
And thou present'st a pure unstainèd prime.
Thou hast passed by the ambush of young days
10 Either not assailed, or victor being charged;
Yet this thy praise cannot be so thy praise,
To tie up envy, evermore enlarged.
    If some suspect of ill masked not thy show,
    Then thou alone kingdoms of hearts shouldst owe.

7 *would be forgot* – wish to be forgotten.

8 *woe* – used as a verb here (see 41.7).

11 *rehearse* – repeat.

Why do you think the world would mock the Friend's love?

---

4 *prove* – show, illustrate.

6 *desert* – (see 49.10)

8 *niggard* – miserly (from Old Norse).

12 *nor me nor you* – neither me nor you (see Sonnet 65).

What do you think the poet is ashamed of – his verse or his life?

71

No longer mourn for me when I am dead
Than you shall hear the surly sullen bell
Give warning to the world that I am fled
From this vile world with vilest worms to dwell.
5   Nay, if you read this line, remember not
The hand that writ it; for I love you so
That I in your sweet thoughts would be forgot
If thinking on me then should make you woe.
O, if, I say, you look upon this verse
10 When I perhaps compounded am with clay,
Do not so much as my poor name rehearse,
But let your love even with my life decay,
        Lest the wise world should look into your moan
        And mock you with me after I am gone.

72

O, lest the world should task you to recite
What merit lived in me that you should love,
After my death, dear love, forget me quite;
For you in me can nothing worthy prove—
5   Unless you would devise some virtuous lie
To do more for me than mine own desert,
And hang more praise upon deceasèd I
Than niggard truth would willingly impart.
O, lest your true love may seem false in this,
10 That you for love speak well of me untrue,
My name be buried where my body is,
And live no more to shame nor me nor you;
        For I am shamed by that which I bring forth,
        And so should you, to love things nothing worth.

4 *choirs* – empty winter trees and the absence of their summer choirs of birds. Perhaps also a reference to ruined monasteries which had begun to decay after the dissolution of the monasteries. The choir was the part of the monastery where the monks sang.

6 *As* – see 66.2.

9 *glowing* – the glowing of the embers when a fire is nearly burnt out.

In **Romeo and Juliet**, Friar Lawrence advises Romeo not to be over-hasty or rash in his love, saying:
'These violent delights have violent ends,
And in their triumph die; like fire and powder,
Which, as they kiss, consume.' (3.4.7)
Which two lines in this sonnet are most similar to Friar Lawrence's words – and why?

Sonnet 74 continues the argument of Sonnet 73.

1 *fell* – cruel, undaunted (see 64.1).

2 *bail* – 1) bail, fee to gain temporary release of a charged prisoner; 2) bale, a sense of sorrow, sadness.

3 *in this line* – 1) in this way; 2) in this verse.

3 *interest* – a powerful friend, e.g. interest at court, who would have been able to obtain bail.

4 *stay* – be remembered, or be kept.

6 *very part* – truest part.

6 *consecrate* – made sacred for, kept especially for.

9 *dregs* – an image taken from brewing, where the dregs in the bottom of beer are the sediment, literally the dead bodies of the brewing yeast organisms.

12 *base* – common, unworthy.

13–14 The value of the body is the spirit which it contains and the spirit can be identified with this poetry which endures, along with you.

Once again the poet staves off his depression by finding immortality in poetry. Compare this sonnet with other sonnets on the same theme (e.g. Sonnet 56).

73

This time of year thou mayst in me behold
When yellow leaves, or none, or few do hang
Upon those boughs which shake against the cold,
Bare ruined choirs, where late the sweet birds sang.
5 In me thou seest the twilight of such day
As after sunset fadeth in the west,
Which by and by blacknight doth take away,
Death's second self that seals up all in rest.
In me thou seest the glowing of such fire
10 That on the ashes of his youth doth lie
As the death-bed whereon it must expire,
Consumed with that which it was nourished by.
    That thou perceiv'st, which makes thy love more strong,
    To love that well which thou must leave ere long.

74

But be contented when that fell arrest
Without all bail shall carry me away.
My life hath in this line some interest,
Which for memorial still with thee shall stay.
5 When thou reviewest this, thou dost review
The very part was consecrate to thee.
The earth can have but earth, which is his due;
My spirit is thine, the better part of me.
So then thou hast but lost the dregs of life,
10 The prey of worms, my body being dead,
The coward conquest of a wretch's knife,
Too base of thee to be rememberèd.
    The worth of that is that which it contains,
    And that is this, and this with thee remains.

2   *Of as* – 'in the same way that that'.
3   *for the peace of you* – for your peace of mind.

6   *filching* – light-fingered, thievish.
6   *his treasure* – the miser's treasure.

9   *Some time* – at times.
10 *clean starved* – completely starved.
12 *Save* – except.
12 *must...be took* – it can only be taken.
13 *pine and surfeit* – alternately strive and overcompensate.
14 *Or...or* – either...or.

Is this a sonnet about love or about flattery?

---

1   *pride* – ornament, gimmick or ideas.

3   *with the time* – with fashion.
4   *compounds strange* – this line would suggest the rivals do not stick to sonnet form for their love poetry.
5   *ever the same* – a curious thing for Shakespeare to say, given the other verse forms he used in poems and plays eleswhere.
6   *weed* – dress, clothes.

10 *argument* – theme; plot; the name given to the brief synopsis at the beginning of a narrative poem.

Do you agree with the poet that the sonnets are 'far from variation or quick change'?

Why do you think the poet finds comfort in the repetitive nature of his verse?

75

So are you to my thoughts as food to life,
Of as sweet-seasoned showers are to the ground;
And for the peace of you I hold such strife
As 'twixt a miser and his wealth is found:
5 Now proud as an enjoyer, and anon
Doubting the filching age will steal his treasure;
Now counting best to be with you alone,
Then bettered that the world may see my pleasure;
Sometime all full with feasting on your sight,
10 And by and by clean starvèd for a look;
Possessing or pursuing no delight
Save what is had or must from you be took.
    Thus do I pine and surfeit day by day,
    Or gluttoning on all, or all away.

76

Why is my verse so barren of new pride,
So far from variation or quick change?
Why, with the time, do I not glance aside
To new-found methods and to compounds strange?
5 Why write I still all one, ever the same,
And keep invention in a noted weed,
That every word doth almost tell my name,
Showing their birth and where they did proceed?
O know, sweet love, I always write of you,
10 And you and love are still my argument;
So all my best is dressing old words new,
Spending again what is already spent;
    For as the sun is daily new and old,
    So is my love, still telling what is told.

This is the first of several sonnets concerned with a Rival Poet.

1 *glass* – mirror.
2 *dial* – sundial.
3 *vacant leaves* – empty pages.
4 *of this book* – from this book. This book will give you an example of what I have said in lines 1 and 2 – 'this learning', that is, 'the passage of time'.
9 *Look...* – make sure you...
10 *blacks* – letters, of black ink; each letter 'wasting' the minutes.
10 *Commit* – write down.
12 Ready to re-acquaint themselves if you read them again years later when the event is forgotten.
13 *look* – 1) remember to do it, as in line 9; 2) look into the book again at a later time.

If this sonnet was written as part of a gift, what exactly would that gift have been? What might have been on it?

1 *invoked* – called upon for inspiration.
3 *alien* – most likely to mean 'other than his own'.
7 *Have added feathers to the learned's wing* – have inspired my rival to surpass his previous excellence. A continuation of the **extended metaphor** (see page 181) in lines 5-6.
10 *born* – 1) born of his inspiration; 2) borne aloft.
11 *but mend the style* – simply improving what is already very good, possibly meaning translators of classical works such as Chapman's **Homer** or Marlowe's **Hero and Leander.**
12 *arts* – the existing ability and subject matter of other poets.
13 *my art* – my learning, skill, pun on heart.
14 *rude* – simple, humble.
14 *ignorance* – unfamiliarity with classical learning.

What is the poet's view of his own poetry in relation to life and art? How does he view his rivals' verse?

Is the poet ashamed of his lack of formal education?

77

Thy glass will show thee how thy beauties wear,
Thy dial how thy precious minutes waste,
The vacant leaves thy mind's imprint will bear,
And of this book this learning mayst thou taste:
5 The wrinkles which thy glass will truly show
Of mouthèd graves will give thee memory;
Thou by thy dial's shady stealth mayst know
Time's thievish progress to eternity;
Look what thy memory cannot contain
10 Commit to these waste blacks, and thou shalt find
Those children nursed, delivered from thy brain,
To take a new acquaintance of thy mind.
    These offices so oft as thou wilt look
    Shall profit thee and much enrich thy book.

78

So oft have I invoked thee for my muse.
And found such fair assistance in my verse,
As every alien pen hath got my use,
And under thee their poesy disperse.
5 Thine eyes, that taught the dumb on high to sing
And heavy ignorance aloft to fly,
Have added feathers to the learned's wing,
And given grace a double majesty.
Yet be most proud of that which I compile,
10 Whose influence is thine and born of thee,
In others' works thou dost but mend the style,
And arts with thy sweet graces gracèd be;
    But thou art all my art, and dost advance
    As high as learning my rude ignorance.

3 *gracious numbers* – verse full of grace.
3 *decayed* – 1) corrupted; 2) worn-out, out of fashion.
5 *argument* – story.

8–14 Introduces the **conceit** (see page 179) that the subject of the poem gives rise to the compliment which is then repaid by the poet, hence the subject pays a debt owed to himself.

11 *afford* – give.

---

2 *spirit* – this word has been interpreted as suggesting that the rival was a poet interested in communicating with the dead, such as Marlowe or Chapman.

7 *saucy barque* – small boat, with a suggestion of impudence.
8 *main* – sea.
8 *wilfully* – deliberately, cheekily. Also a suggestion of the poet's name (see 57.13).
10 *soundless* – impossible to tell how deep.
11 *wrecked* – Quarto has 'wrack't', with a suggestion of torture (on the rack).
14 *decay* – his love leads to his downfall. Pursuing the **metaphor** (see page 181) of the wrecked or abandoned boat, the poet's love/boat can only be wrecked if it puts to sea in the first place.

Do you think the poet feels his rivals' verse is stylistically superior? Why (not)?

79

Whilst I alone did call upon thy aid
My verse alone had all thy gentle grace;
But now my gracious numbers are decayed,
And my sick muse doth give another place.
5   I grant, sweet love, thy lovely argument
Deserves the travail of a worthier pen,
Yet what of thee thy poet doth invent
He robs thee of, and pays it thee again.
He lends thee virtue, and he stole that word
10   From thy behaviour; beauty doth he give,
And found it in thy cheek: he can afford
No praise to thee but what in thee doth live.
     Then thank him not for that which he doth say,
     Since what he owes thee thou thyself dost pay.

80

O how I faint when I of you do write,
Knowing a better spirit doth use your name,
And in the praise thereof spends all his might,
To make me tongue-tied, speaking of your fame!
5   But since your worth, wide as the ocean is,
The humble as the proudest sail doth bear,
My saucy barque, inferior far to his,
On your broad main doth wilfully appear.
Your shallowest help will hold me up afloat,
10   Whilst he upon your soundless deep doth ride;
Or, being wrecked, I am a worthless boat,
He of tall building and of goodly pride.
     Then if he thrive and I be cast away,
     The worst was this: my love was my decay.

1–2   Either I will outlive you or you me.

7   *common grave* – 1) ordinary, run-of-the-mill grave or 2) a mass (communal) grave, the fate of paupers and plague victims.

9   *gentle* – also 'genteel', recalling 'common' in line 7.

11   *your being shall rehearse* – shall recreate your spirit.

14   *even...* meaning 'that is to say'.

---

4   *fair subject* – a difficult **pun** (see page 182) because the dedication is not usually about the subject of the book, but about its dedicatee or patron. If, however, the 'book' is an image for the beloved, and the beloved is the Patron, the confusion is dissolved.

8   *fresher stamp* – a new, younger poet – suggests the fresh face of the young poet and echoes the 'book' of line 4.

8   *time-bettering days* – modern days improve on time gone by.

10   *strainèd touches* – ornaments or fashionable features.

10   *rhetoric* – rhetoric (the studied art of persuasion in speech or writing) suggests that the new verse is learned.

11   *truly fair* – pure, inherent beauty.

11   *sympathized* – portrayed.

13   *gross painting* – he compares the other poets' fine rhetoric to cosmetic make-up (see Sonnets 67, 68 and 83 for his opinion of cosmetics!).

14   *blood* – colour, beauty (see 63.3 and 67.10).

In what ways is the Friend beautiful?

What does the poet criticize about his rivals' poetic style? (Compare Sonnet 80.)

Does this sonnet suggest that Shakespeare envied his rivals?

81

Or shall I live your epitaph to make,
Or you survive in earth when I am rotten.
From hence your memory death cannot take,
Although in me each part will be forgotten.
5   Your name from hence immortal life shall have,
Though I, once gone, to all the world must die.
The earth can yield me but a common grave
When you entombèd in men's eyes shall lie.
Your monument shall be my gentle verse,
10   Which eyes not yet created shall o'er-read,
And tongues to be your being shall rehearse
When all the breathers of this world are dead.
    You still shall live – such virtue hath my pen –
    Where breath most breathes, even in the mouths of men.

82

I grant thou wert not married to my muse,
And therefore mayst without attaint o'erlook
The dedicated words which writers use
Of their fair subject, blessing every book.
5   Thou art as fair in knowledge as in hue,
Finding thy worth a limit past my praise,
And therefore art enforced to seek anew,
Some fresher stamp of the time-bettering days.
And do so, love; yet when they have devised,
10   What strainèd touches rhetoric can lend,
Thou, truly fair, wert truly sympathized
In true plain words by thy true-telling friend;
    And their gross painting might be better used
    Where cheeks need blood: in thee it is abused.

2 *painting* – make-up, ornaments, or rhetorical flourishes in poetry.

4 *tender of a poet's debt* – suggesting poems in return for patronage. Also suggesting an insincerity in the 'love' they profess (see 10).

5 *slept in your report* – refrained from praising/writing about you.

6 *extant* – alive, in existence.

7 *modern quill* – fashionable poet (see 78.7).

10 *most my glory being dumb* – perhaps his finest works because they are too sincere, truthful and personal to publish.

10 *dumb* – Quarto has 'dombe' to show full rhyme with tomb, allowing a word-play on death (doom) and silence (dumb) (see 86.6).

In line 12 the poet suggests that other poets aim to make the subject live in their verse, but what does he think they actually achieve?

Is there an implied criticism of the Friend for accepting inferior verse?

1–2 Whoever it is who says most about you can say no more than that you are yourself alone.

3 *immured* – walled in.

3 *store* – whole supply.

3–4 The poet is suggesting that the Friend already embodies the only things he could be compared with.

5 *Lean penury* – poverty, miserliness.

5–6 It is a miserly, mean poet who cannot add some small enhancement to his subject.

8 *so* – 'it so...'

10 Without detracting from what nature has created.

14 *fond on praise* – drunk on praise. Hence, because he loves to hear himself praised, he will accept any old rubbish, so long as it praises him, thus encouraging bad poets!

What is the curse in line 13?

83

    I never saw that you did painting need,
    And therefore to your fair no painting set.
    I found – or thought I found – you did exceed
    The barren tender of a poet's debt;
5   And therefore have I slept in your report:
    That you yourself, being extant, well might show
    How far a modern quill doth come too short,
    Speaking of worth, what worth in you doth grow.
    This silence for my sin you did impute,
10 Which shall be most my glory being dumb,
    For I impair not beauty, being mute,
    When others would give life, and bring a tomb.
        There lives more life in one of your fair eyes
        Than both your poets can in praise devise.

84

    Who is it that says most which can say more
    Than this rich praise: that you alone are you,
    In whose confine immured is the store
    Which should example where your equal grew?
5   Lean penury within that pen doth dwell
    That to his subject lends not some small glory;
    But he that writes of you, if he can tell
    That you are you, so dignifies his story.
    Let him but copy what in you is writ,
10 Not making worse what nature made so clear,
    And as such counterpart shall fame his wit,
    Making his style admirèd every where.
        You to your beauteous blessing add a curse,
        Being fond on praise, which makes your praises worse.

1 *tongue-tide* – silent, dumb.

2 *compiled* – organized, in formal verses.

3 *Reserve thy character* – preserve them in writing.

4 *filed* – organized, put in ranks.

6 *unlettered clerk* – (illiterate) lay assistant to the parish priest.

7 *hymn* – Quarto has 'Himne' – a visual **pun** (see page 182) between 'hymn' and every 'Him' meaning every other poet.

14 *dumb* – (see 83.10)

What is the poet saying about his rivals' poetry compared with his own?

1 *full sail* – (see 80.8)

2 *Bound for the prize* – suggesting the capture of a vessel at sea.

3 *inhearse* – entomb (coined by Shakespeare for this poem).

6 *pitch* – from falconry, highest flying altitude.

6 *dead* – here 'dead' is used in place of 'dumb' in the familiar phrase 'struck dumb' (see 83.10).

7 *his compeers* – his equals, his fellows.

7 *by night* – possibly spirits of dead writers?

8 *astonishèd* – left as though speechless.

9 *affable familiar* – friendly spirit. A 'familiar' was a companion, sometimes a devil.

10 *gulls him* – 1) dupes him, cons him; 2) crams his gorge with poetry, as a gull or a gannet crams its young with food.

12 *sick of any fear* – fear generates a sick feeling.

13 *countenance* – face.

13 *line* – verse.

14 *enfeebled* – made it seem pathetic in style.

What has enfeebled the poet's verse?

'Spirits', 'familiar ghosts' and 'compeers by night' conjure up images of the rival poet in conference with dead writers. This could be: 1) an ironic way of suggesting the rival poet's work is derivative; 2) a way of expressing sincere admiration for the rival poet.

Do you think the praise of the rival poet's verse is ironic or sincere?

85

My tongue-tide muse with manners keeps her still
While comments of your praise, richly compiled,
Reserve thy character with golden quill
And precious phrase by all the muses filed.
5   I think good thoughts whilst others write good words,
And like unlettered clerk still cry 'Amen'
To every hymn that able spirit affords
In polished form of well-refinèd pen.
Hearing you praised I say ''Tis so, 'tis true,'
10   And to the most of praise add something more;
But that is in my thought, whose love to you,
Though words come hindmost, holds his rank before.
     Then others for the breath of words respect,
     Me for my dumb thoughts, speaking in effect.

86

Was it the proud full sail of his great verse
Bound for the prize of all-too-precious you
That did my ripe thoughts in my brain inhearse,
Making their tomb the womb wherein they grew?
5   Was it his spirit, by spirits taught to write
Above a mortal pitch, that struck me dead?
No, neither he nor his compeers by night
Giving him aid my verse astonishèd.
He nor that affable familiar ghost
10   Which nightly gulls him with intelligence,
As victors, of my silence cannot boast;
I was not sick of any fear from thence.
     But when your countenance filled up his line,
     Then lacked I matter; that enfeebled mine.

1 *too dear* – 1) too costly; 2) too much beloved.

2 *estimate* – 1) 'market value'; 2) value in which he is held by the poet.

3 *charter* – see Sonnet 58.

4 *bonds* – legal commitments, but also ropes or chains.

4 *determinate* – limited, possibly meaning 'finished'.

6 *that riches* – his 'holding' the beloved, or that which is 'granted' in line 5.

6 *deserving* – what he as a lover deserves, or another reference to social standing see 'desert' (see 49.10).

8 *patent* – legal term, right of ownership or bond.

8 *swerving* – reverting to its original owner.

10 *mistaking* – with a play on 'gav'st' and 'taking'.

11 *misprision* – misconstrued, misunderstood, mistaken.

> *What is the effect of the feminine rhymes?*

7 *attainted* – condemned for treason.

12 *double vantage* – make advantage for both the scornful lover and thereby for himself.

> *Compare this sonnet with Sonnet 49.*

87

Farewell – thou art too dear for my possessing,
And like enough thou know'st thy estimate.
The charter of thy worth gives thee releasing;
My bonds in thee are all determinate.
5 For how do I hold thee but by thy granting,
And for that riches where is my deserving?
The cause of this fair gift in me is wanting,
And so my patent back again is swerving.
Thyself thou gav'st, thy own worth then not knowing,
10 Or me, to whom thou gav'st it else mistaking;
So thy great gift, upon misprision growing,
Comes home again, on better judgement making.
    Thus have I had thee as a dream doth flatter:
    In sleep a king but waking no such matter.

88

When thou shalt be disposed to set me light
And place my merit in the eye of scorn,
Upon thy side, against myself I'll fight,
And prove thee virtuous, though thou art forsworn.
5 With mine own weakness being best acquainted,
Upon thy part I can set down a story
Of faults concealed, wherein I am attainted,
That thou in losing me shall win much glory;
And I by this will be a gainer too;
10 For bending all my loving thoughts on thee,
The injuries that to myself I do,
Doing thee vantage, double vantage me.
    Such is my love, to thee I so belong,
    That for thy right myself will bear all wrong.

1   *for* – on account of, because of.

3   *halt* – limp.

6   *To set a form upon* – to make clear, to explain, to give body to [what change it is you desire].
8   *acquaintance strangle* – kill all signs of recognition.
8   *look strange* – not acknowledge you in passing.
9   *thy walks* – where you habitually walk.
11   *profane* – sacrilegious, unworthy.
12   *haply* – by chance.
13   *vow debate* – declare enmity, make war.

---

1   *wilt* – wish.
2   *bent* – inclined, determined.

4   *drop* – a much stronger word than it would seem today, used to illustrate how ill fortune can unexpectedly descend on people as though from a clear blue sky.
6   *rearward* – rearguard – a strong and dangerous force, left at the back of a seemingly defeated army, which can still mount a surprise attack.
8   *purposed* – already decided, predetermined.

11   *in the onset* – in the beginning, at first.

13   *strains* – 1) musical tunes; 2) types, essences, elements.
13   *which now seem woe* – which now seem catastrophic.

Is this a pessimistic or an optimistic poem?

89

Say that thou didst forsake me for some fault,
And I will comment upon that offence;
Speak of my lameness, and I straight will halt,
Against thy reasons making no defence.
5 Thou canst not, love, disgrace me half so ill,
To set a form upon desirèd change,
As I'll my self disgrace, knowing thy will.
I will acquaintance strangle and look strange,
Be absent from thy walks, and in my tongue
10 Thy sweet belovèd name no more shall dwell,
Lest I, too much profane, should do it wrong,
And haply of our old acquaintance tell.
    For thee, against myself I'll vow debate;
    For I must ne'er love him whom thou dost hate.

90

Then hate me when thou wilt, if ever, now,
Now while the world is bent my deeds to cross,
Join with the spite of fortune, make me bow,
And do not drop in for an after-loss.
5 Ah do not, when my heart hath scaped this sorrow,
Come in the rearward of a conquered woe;
Give not a windy night a rainy morrow,
To linger out a purposed overthrow.
If thou wilt leave me, do not leave me last,
10 When other petty griefs have done their spite,
But in the onset come, so I shall taste
At first the very worst of fortune's might,
    And other strains of woe, which now seem woe,
    Compared with loss of thee, will not seem so.

1   *birth* – social status.

3   *new-fangled ill* – made in unattractive new fashion.
4   *hawks and hounds* – falcons and hunting hounds.
4   *horse* – stable full of horses. Here a means of transport rather than an allusion simply to hunting.
5   *humour* – temperament (see 45.1) or, possibly, mood.
5   *adjunct* – corresponding, associated.
7   *measure* – 1) the purpose of my verse (as in 'numbers'); 2) like clothes which do not fit my person, these attributes do not fit my personality.
8   *general best* – overwhelming, all-inclusive best.

---

1   *But* – the argument flows from Sonnet 91.

4   *depends* – strictly, 'hangs from', evoking the image, 'hanging from the thread of thy love'.
5   *Then* – therefore.

8   *humour* – mood, inclination (see 91.5).
9   *vex* – trouble, annoy.

11   *happy title* – blessed entitlement, given by God or fortune, echoing aristocratic honour or title such as 'Lord' or 'Earl', given by the Queen.
11   *inconstant* – changing, vacillating.
13   *blessèd fair* – full of holy beauty, beautiful in righteousness.
14   *yet I know it not* – yet I will not be aware of it.

Will the poet not be upset by the Friend's frequent changes of mind?

91

Some glory in their birth, some in their skill,
Some in their wealth, some in their body's force,
Some in their garments (though new-fangled ill);
Some in their hawks and hounds, some in their horse,
5 And every humour hath his adjunct pleasure
Wherein it finds a joy above the rest.
But these particulars are not my measure;
All these I better in one general best.
Thy love is better than high birth to me,
10 Richer than wealth, prouder than garments' cost,
Of more delight than hawks or horses be,
And having thee of all men's pride I boast,
    Wretched in this alone: that thou mayst take
    All this away, and me most wretched make.

92

But do thy worst to steal thyself away,
For term of life thou art assurèd mine,
And life no longer than thy life will stay,
For it depends upon that love of thine.
5 Then need I not to fear the worst of wrongs
When in the least of them my life hath end.
I see a better state to me belongs
Than that which on thy humour doth depend.
Thou canst not vex me with inconstant mind,
10 Since that my life on thy revolt doth lie.
O, what a happy title do I find –
Happy to have thy love, happy to die!
    But what's so blessèd fair that fears no blot?
    Thou mayst be false, and yet I know it not.

1   *So* – thus, following on from Sonnet 92, presumably.

1   *supposing* – The poet is alive, therefore the lover is true (see Sonnet 92).

3   *altered new* – 1) recently changed; 2) a new sacrifice on love's shrine, inferred from a **pun** on 'altar' (see page 182).

5   *eye* – 1) look, the way you look at me; 2) possibly a vulgar expression for the female sexual organ.

8   *strange* – unknown before.

13   *Eve's apple* – see biblical story of Adam and Eve. The apple was tempting to Eve because it appeared to be good to eat, yet it grew on the 'tree of knowledge'; its 'good' appearance was deceptive.

14   *sweet virtue* – ironic, and therefore the virtue is the opposite of 'sweet.'

14   *answer* – correspond to.

What makes the metaphor of the apple from the tree of knowledge (line 13) so apt for this poem (see Sonnets 90–92)?

---

2   Who do not do what their appearance suggests they will do. Lines 1 and 2 can be read in various ways: 1) honourable: who look dangerous but behave well; 2) unreliable: who do not act in the way one is led to expect they will; 3) hypocritical: who do one thing while appearing to do another.

3–4   Such people who disturb other people emotionally ('moving others') are themselves indifferent, as cold as 'stone'.

6   *husband* – keep safe, save, do not spend (i.e. carefully protect beauty – 'nature's riches' – from what they give away).

7   *faces* – features. Lines 1–6 suggest overtones of self-possession as well as their features.

8   *but stewards* – only custodians, managers.

8   *their excellence* – ambiguous 1) 'their excellence' could refer to those who are lords and owners with the 'stewards' being other people who tend to them; 2) or 'their excellence' refers to the temporary 'excellence' mere stewards hold.

9–10   A flower which blooms in summer gives sweetness to that season even though all it gives to itself is one season's life and then death.

12   *outbraves his dignity* – becomes morally superior to him; 'weed' can mean costume as well as wild plant; 'outbraves' means surpasses, and can also be read as 'is braver than'; and 'dignity' can refer to an outer and inner state.

For an extended activity on this sonnet, see page 167.

93

So shall I live supposing thou art true
Like a deceivèd husband; so love's face,
May still seem love to me, though altered new –
Thy looks with me, thy heart in other place.
5 For there can live no hatred in thine eye,
Therefore in that I cannot know thy change.
In many's looks, the false heart's history
Is writ in moods and frowns and wrinkles strange;
But heaven in thy creation did decree
10 That in thy face sweet love should ever dwell;
Whate'er thy thoughts or thy heart's workings be,
Thy looks should nothing thence but sweetness tell.
    How like Eve's apple doth thy beauty grow
    If thy sweet virtue answer not thy show!

94

They that have power to hurt and will do none,
That do not do the thing they most do show,
Who moving others are themselves as stone,
Unmovèd, cold, and to temptation slow –
5 They rightly do inherit heaven's graces,
And husband nature's riches from expense;
They are the lords and owners of their faces,
Others but stewards of their excellence.
The summer's flower is to the summer sweet
10 Though to itself it only live and die,
But if that flower with base infection meet
The basest weed outbraves his dignity;
    For sweetest things turn sourest by their deeds:
    Lilies that fester smell far worse than weeds.

2　*canker* – this could either be the canker worm, destroying the rose in bud, or a dog-rose sprouting from a fragrant, cultivated rose bush (see 1.11, 35.4, 54.5, 70.7).

3　*spot* – to mar, to blemish, to corrupt – a stain, as in sin.

6　*lascivious* – sexually depraved or explicit.

6　*Naming thy name* – 1) referring to a dedication before a work; 2) possibly using the same nickname, such as 'the Rose'. The name itself should be praise (as earlier references to the beloved as inspiration).

9　*mansion* – the subject's body.

12　*fair* – virtue.

13　*large privilege* – freedom.

14　*hardest knife* – possibly a commonplace Elizabethan adage. Certainly a quibble on the male sexual organ and venereal disease, implying habitual promiscuity in the Friend.

Does the sexual reference in line 14 have a purpose, or is it just gratuitous?

1　*wantonness* – levity, sexual licence.

2　*gentle sport* – a synonym for wantonness, perhaps emphasizing the supposedly harmless nature of it.

3　*loved of more and less* – loved by greater and more humble persons, i.e. everyone.

4　*faults* – those who commit 'faults' with the Friend.

8　*translated* – transformed.

8　*deemed* – believed.

11　*gazers* – those who look on him, possibly followers.

13–14　Identical to lines 13–14 of Sonnet 36.

95

How sweet and lovely dost thou make the shame
Which, like a canker in the fragrant rose,
Doth spot the beauty of thy budding name!
O, in what sweets dost thou thy sins enclose!
5   That tongue that tells the story of thy days,
Making lascivious comments on thy sport,
Cannot dispraise, but in a kind of praise,
Naming thy name, blesses an ill report.
O, what a mansion have those vices got
10   Which for their habitation chose out thee,
Where beauty's veil doth cover every blot
And all things turn to fair that eyes can see!
    Take heed, dear heart, of this large privilege:
    The hardest knife ill used doth lose his edge.

96

Some say thy fault is youth, some wantonness,
Some say thy grace is youth and gentle sport.
Both grace and faults are loved of more and less;
Thou mak'st faults graces, that to thee resort.
5   As on the finger of a thronèd queen,
The basest jewel will be well esteemed,
So are those errors that in thee are seen
To truths translated and for true things deemed.
How many lambs might the stern wolf betray
10   If like a lamb he could his looks translate!
How many gazers mightst thou lead away
If thou wouldst use the strength of all thy state!
    But do not so: I love thee in such sort
    As, thou being mine, mine is thy good report.

2 *fleeting* – swiftly passing, short-lived.

4–5 *old December's* – traditional personification of the year, December being its old age, January its infancy.

4 *summer's time* – labour. Summer, as an expectant mother, at the point of birth, her 'time'. Autumn will be the actual birth. (See **personification**, page 182.)

6 *big* – pregnant.

7 *wanton* – indulgent.

7 *burden* – offspring.

7 *prime* – spring.

8 *decease* – death.

9 *issue* – child, the result of the pregnancy.

9 *unfathered fruit* – illegitimate children who, like orphans, have no hope of inheritance.

11 *wait on thee* – 1) wait for thee...to return; 2) attend thee, wherever 'summer' is now.

12 *the very birds...* – even the birds...

---

2 *pied* – black and white – the white blossom against the black winter twigs and branches; or simply dappled, variegated.

4 *Saturn* – Roman god of agriculture or vegetation, which is renewed in vigour each year.

5 *lays* – songs.

6 *hue* – colour, shade or form, relating to 'different'.

7 *summer's story tell* – tell a tale appropriate to summer.

8 *lap* – comparing the leafy part of the plant to the female sexual organ, from which the flower grows.

10 *vermilion* – red.

11 *sweet* – an essence, a smell.

11 *figures* – letters/pictures.

12 *Drawn* – a pun on drawing a picture, and following on necessarily, as does a carriage drawn by a horse.

97

How like a winter hath my absence been
From thee, the pleasure of the fleeting year!
What freezings have I felt, what dark days seen,
What old December's bareness everywhere!
5 And yet this time removed was summer's time,
And teeming autumn big with rich increase,
Bearing the wanton burden of the prime
Like widowed wombs after their lord's decease.
Yet this abundant issue seemed to me
10 But hope of orphans, and unfathered fruit,
For summer and his pleasures wait on thee,
And thou away, the very birds are mute;
    Or if they sing, 'tis with so dull a cheer
    That leaves look pale, dreading the winter's near.

98

From you I have been absent in the spring,
When proud-pied April, dressed in all his trim,
Hath put a spirit of youth in everything,
That heavy Saturn laughed and leapt with him.
5 Yet nor the lays of birds nor the sweet smell
Of different flowers in odour and in hue,
Could make me any summer's story tell,
Or from their proud lap pluck them where they grew;
Nor did I wonder at the lily's white,
10 Nor praise the deep vermilion in the rose,
They were but sweet, but figures of delight
Drawn after you, you pattern of all those;
    Yet seemed it winter still, and, you away,
    As with your shadow I with these did play.

1   *forward* – insolent.
1   *chide* – scold, criticize, accuse.
2   *Sweet thief* – 1) thief who is sweet; 2) thief of 'a sweet' (see note below).
2   *thy sweet* – nature, quintessence (see 98.11).
3   *the purple pride* – here Shakespeare makes colour and smell virtually identical (see 98.6).
5   *veins* – 1) blood vessels; 2) rivulets.
5   *grossly* – impertinently, greedily.
6   *condemned* – sentenced to death.
7   *marjoram* – an aromatic herb.
7   *stolen* – pronounced as one syllable (stol'n).
7   *fearfully* – reflecting their 'shame' and 'despair'.
11 *But* – except.

3   *fury* – poetic force, more than anger.
3   *base* – dark (see 33.5).
6   *gentle numbers* – noble verses, as opposed to base songs.
7   *lays* – songs.
7   *esteem* – pay attention, admiringly.
8   *argument* – a decent plot.
10 *If* – to see if.
10 *graven* – engraved, carved, drawn.
11 *satire* – in Quarto given italics and capital. 1) satyr – mythical creature, half goat, half man; 2) satire. A satire is a literary work which holds something or someone up to public ridicule.
12 *time's spoils* – 1) booty, spoils of war: 2) spoiling, destruction (see 65.12). Shakespeare appears to be saying that, if Time has had the temerity to plant wrinkles on the beloved's brow, his muse should retaliate by satirising Time, i.e. belittling his power to despoil beauty.
14 *prevent'st* – thwart, forestall.

What effect has the Young Man's absence had on the poet?

What do you notice about the change in tone, compared with Sonnets 88–96?

99

The forward violet thus did I chide:
Sweet thief, whence didst thou steal thy sweet that smells,
If not from my love's breath? The purple pride
Which on thy soft cheek for complexion dwells
5   In my love's veins thou hast too grossly dyed.
The lily I condemnèd for thy hand,
And buds of marjoram had stolen thy hair,
The roses fearfully on thorns did stand,
One blushing shame, another white despair;
10 A third, nor red nor white, had stolen of both,
And to his robb'ry had annexed thy breath;
But for his theft in pride of all his growth
A vengeful canker ate him up to death.
     More flowers I noted, yet I none could see
15   But sweet or colour it had stolen from thee.

100

Where art thou, muse, that thou forget'st so long
To speak of that which gives thee all thy might?
Spend'st thou thy fury on some worthless song,
Dark'ning thy power to lend base subjects light?
5 Return, forgetful muse, and straight redeem
In gentle numbers time so idly spent;
Sing to the ear that doth thy lays esteem
And gives thy pen both skill and argument.
Rise, resty muse, my love's sweet face survey
10 If time have any wrinkle graven there.
If any, be a satire to decay
And make time's spoils despisèd everywhere.
     Give my love fame faster than time wastes life;
     So, thou prevent'st his scythe, and crookèd knife.

2 *dyed* – or died.

3 *on my love depends* – his love is not the subject, but his own feeling. Truth and beauty are equally dependent upon it, for through neglecting of his love, truth has died.

5 *haply* – naturally, typically.

6 *colour fixed* – pure colour – presumably, white, which contains no colour. Truth is simple, with nothing added.

7 *pencil* – not a modern, colourless lead pencil but an extremely fine brush used by miniaturists, and, ironically, for make-up.

8 *intermixed* – 'best' can no longer be so if mixed.

9 *he* – i.e. truth.

13 *do thy office, muse* – an injunction, as in line 5, for the muse to make an answer.

What does the poet expect from the muse in lines 13–14?

---

1 *strengthened* – two syllables – 'strength-ned'.

3 *merchandized* – turned into something saleable.

6 *wont* – in the habit of, willing to.

6 *lays* – songs.

7 *Philomel* – poetic name for the nightingale, from the Greek myth of Philomela who was turned into a nightingale by the gods. Philomel is 'her' elsewhere.

8 *his pipe* – the Quarto reading.

11 *burdens* – 'weights down', with a punning reference (see page 182) to 'bourdon', an old musical term for something which runs throughout a piece of music (either a continuous bass note or a refrain repeated at the end of each verse of a song).

12 *sweets* – pleasures, desires (see 95, 98.11 and 99.2).

13 *her* – Philomel.

13 *sometime* – for the time being.

14 *dull you* – 1) bore you; 2) diminish you, do you down.

Contrast the music of line 7 with that of line 12.

101

O truant muse, what shall be thy amends
For thy neglect of truth in beauty dyed?
Both truth and beauty on my love depends;
So dost thou too, and therein dignified.
5   Make answer muse. Wilt thou not haply say
'Truth needs no colour with his colour fixed,
Beauty no pencil, beauty's truth to lay,
But best is best if never intermixed'?
Because he needs no praise wilt thou be dumb?
10   Excuse not silence so, for't lies in thee
To make him much outlive a gilded tomb:
And to be praised of ages yet to be.
        Then do thy office, muse; I teach thee how
        To make him seem long hence, as he shows now.

102

My love is strengthened, though more weak in seeming.
I love not less, though less the show appear.
That love is merchandized whose rich esteeming
The owner's tongue doth publish everywhere.
5   Our love was new and then but in the spring
When I was wont to greet it with my lays;
As Philomel in summer's front doth sing,
And stops his pipe in growth of riper days –
Not that the summer is less pleasant now
10   Than when her mournful hymns did hush the night,
But that wild music burdens every bough,
And sweets grown common lose their dear delight.
        Therefore like her I sometime hold my tongue,
        Because I would not dull you with my song.

3 *bare* – links with *pride* (line 2) which means 'rich dress' and *poverty* (line 1) which implies 'rags'. The poet is destitute of ideas or *argument*.

4 *Than* – Quarto has 'then' throughout this poem – in Shakespeare's time the two words *then* and *than* had not yet separated.

5 *no more* – 1) no longer; 2) nothing more.

6 *glass* – mirror.

7–8 *blunt* – a synonym of 'dulling' (see 102.14).

9 *then* – therefore (see note 4 above).

9 *mend* – improve.

10 *mar* – spoil, damage.

11 *pass* – purpose, end.

> **What does the poet mean by 'overgoes my blunt invention quite' in line 7?**

---

2 eye / *eyde* – often condemned by critics as clumsy or ugly.

5 *turned* – one syllable, to rhyme with burned.

9 *dial* – clock. A mechanical clock early enough for Shakespeare to have seen in a rich household would have had only an hour hand, hence the especially slow motion.

10 *Steal* – creep.

10–11 *still doth stand, Hath motion* – the skin ages imperceptibly, like the hands of a clock move – they seem still, yet we know they are in motion. A clever conceit, suggesting a paradox and also revealing clearly that things are not always as they seem. (See **conceit**, page 179 and **paradox**, page 181.)

11 *sweet hue* – fair complexion (see 98.6).

13 *age unbred* – ages yet to come.

> **Why is the word 'steal' so appropriate in line 10?**

103

Alack, what poverty my muse brings forth
That, having such a scope to show her pride,
The argument all bare is of more worth
Than when it hath my added praise beside!
5 O blame me not if I no more can write!
Look in your glass and there appears a face
That overgoes my blunt invention quite,
Dulling my lines and doing me disgrace.
Were it not sinful then, striving to mend,
10 To mar the subject that before was well? –
For to no other pass my verses tend
Than of your graces and of your gifts to tell.
    And more, much more, than in my verse can sit
    Your own glass shows you when you look in it.

104

To me, fair friend, you never can be old;
For as you were when first your eye I eyde,
Such seems your beauty still. Three winters cold,
Have from the forests shook three summers' pride;
5 Three beauteous springs to yellow Autumn turned
In process of the seasons have I seen,
Three April perfumes in three hot Junes burned
Since first I saw you fresh, which yet are green.
Ah yet doth beauty, like a dial hand,
10 Steal from his figure, and no pace perceived;
So your sweet hue, which methinks still doth stand,
Hath motion, and mine eye may be deceived.
    For fear of which, hear this, thou age unbred:
    Ere you were born was beauty's summer dead.

1 *idolatry* – the biblical sin of worshipping a false god.
2 *idol* – a statue or image.

5 *today, tomorrow* – Quarto has 'today, tomorrow' to give the sense of 'kind to the present, kind to the future'.

11 *spent* – used up, meaning he cannot accomplish the 'change', or think of any more words to add to 'Fair, kind and true'. Implies a sense of waste, especially sexual exhaustion.
12 *Three themes in one* – echoing the language of the Christian Trinity – 'God the Father, God the Son and God the Holy Ghost. One God, three-in-one.'

What is the poet trying to prove through his reference to the Christian Trinity?

1 *chronicle* – historical record.
1 *wasted* – irretrievably gone.
2 *wights* – creatures, used affectionately of women, here the 'ladies dead'. Archaic even then, but appropriate to the theme of the sonnet.
5 *blazon* – a heraldic term, originally meaning coat-of-arms.
6 These physical features were typically singled out for praise in courtly verse.
10 *prefiguring* – drawing in advance.
11 *divining* – also foretelling. Quarto has the old French spelling 'devining', which suggests prediction or foretelling, rather than any more sinister supernatural contact (OED).

105

Let not my love be called idolatry,
Nor my belovèd as an idol show,
Since all alike my songs and praises be
To one, of one, still such, and ever so.
5 Kind is my love today, tomorrow kind,
Still constant in a wondrous excellence,
Therefore my verse, to constancy confined,
One thing expressing, leaves out difference.
'Fair, kind, and true' is all my argument,
10 'Fair, kind, and true' varying to other words,
And in this change is my invention spent,
Three themes in one, which wondrous scope affords.
    Fair, kind, and true have often lived alone,
    Which three till now never kept seat in one.

106

When in the chronicle of wasted time
I see descriptions of the fairest wights,
And beauty making beautiful old rhyme
In praise of ladies dead and lovely knights;
5 Then in the blazon of sweet beauty's best,
Of hand, of foot, of lip, of eye, of brow,
I see their antique pen would have expressed
Ev'n such a beauty as you master now.
So all their praises are but prophecies
10 Of this our time, all you prefiguring,
And for they looked but with divining eyes,
They had not skill enough your worth to sing:
    For we which now behold these present days
    Have eyes to wonder, but lack tongues to praise.

3   *lease* – 1) right of renting; 2) time.

4   *confined doom* – 1) mortality; 2) prediction confined to; 3) a sentence of imprisonment.

5   *mortal moon* – it dies each month and is born again as a 'new moon'. Some critics have suggested it refers to the moon-shaped Spanish Armada of 1588, or to Queen Elizabeth's Grand Climacteric. This was her 63rd year, thought to be a dangerous phase of life because it is the product of the mystical numbers 7 and 9. It may also refer to an illness of the Queen's or to her death in 1603.

6   *sad augùrs* – solemn prophets, serious readers of the future.

6   *presage* – literally, 'foreknowing'.

8   *peace proclaims olives* – olive branches are a biblical symbol of peace.

9   *the drops* – possibly a dose of medicine, or balm.

9   *balmy* – healing.

10 *subscribes* – submits.

12 *speechless tribes* – possibly the 'tribes' of writers whose dull verse will soon be forgotten.

Note how Shakespeare uses public events to mirror and magnify his relationship with the Friend. What is the effect of this?

---

1   *character* – write down.

2   *figured* – drawn.

5   *sweet boy* – one of only two similar references in the sonnets (see Sonnet 126).

8   *hallowed* – sanctified, made holy or sacred.

10 *dust and injury* – 1) the grime and pain of life's journey; 2) possibly an echo of the burial service ('ashes to ashes, dust to dust').

13 *the first conceit of love* – The words conceit and conceive come from the same root (see also **Conceit** page 179).

14 Often taken to mean that 'love may continue fresh in older people'.

In what different ways might love be fresh in line 9?

How does Shakespeare suggest that love might cheat death?

107

Not mine own fears nor the prophetic soul
Of the wide world dreaming on things to come
Can yet the lease of my true love control,
Supposed as forfeit to a confined doom.
5 The mortal moon hath her eclipse endured,
And the sad augurs mock their own presage,
Incertainties now crown themselves assured
And peace proclaims olives of endless age.
Now with the drops of this most balmy time
10 My love looks fresh, and death to me subscribes,
Since spite of him I'll live in this poor rhyme,
While he insults o'er dull and speechless tribes;
        And thou in this shalt find thy monument
        When tyrants' crests and tombs of brass are spent.

108

What's in the brain that ink may character
Which hath not figured to thee my true spirit?
What's new to speak, what now to register,
That may express my love or thy dear merit?
5 Nothing, sweet boy; but yet like prayers divine
I must each day say o'er the very same,
Counting no old thing old, thou mine, I thine,
Even as when first I hallowed thy fair name.
So that eternal love in love's fresh case
10 Weighs not the dust and injury of age,
Nor gives to necessary wrinkles place,
But makes antiquity for aye his page,
        Finding the first conceit of love there bred
        Where time and outward form would show it dead.

2   *to qualify* – to define (as false).

8   *stain* – see 33.14.
9   *reigned* – Quarto has 'raigned' – a **pun** (see page 182) on rain/reign.
10 *kind* – possibly a **pun** (see page 182) on 'types' and 'kindred'.

In line 10 and elsewhere in the collection, 'blood' can mean several different things. Which possibilities fit? How does each affect the poem overall?

2   *motley* – a clown, after their traditional costume made of 'motley', a bright and multi-coloured cloth.
3   *Gored* – 1) wounded; 2) added 'gores', triangular pieces of cloth to my coat, thus making motley; 3) dishonoured, a gore being a heraldic sign for dishonour.
4   *old offences* – possibly 1) offences he himself has committed; 2) old offences which have been committed since the world began.
5   *truth* – 1) verity; 2) trust, constancy.
6   *Askance* – 1) 'from an odd angle', usually thought of as 'with the head tilted to one side' 2) see 49.9 'ensconce'.
6   *by all above* – 1) by heaven; 2) on account of what I have said above.
7   *blenches* – glances, from looking askance; 2) a trick, imposition or cheat; 3) to make white (hence, by inference, 'pure') from a cookery term for dipping almonds in scalding water to remove their dark skins.
8   *worse essays* – from French *essai*, 'trials' or 'attempts'.
9   Receive from me something that will last forever.
10 *grind* – the **metaphor** (see page 181) of sharpening implies a sexual innuendo.

109

O never say that I was false of heart,
Though absence seemed my flame to qualify –
As easy might I from my self depart
As from my soul, which in thy breast doth lie.
5 That is my home of love. If I have ranged,
Like him that travels I return again,
Just to the time, not with the time exchanged,
So that myself bring water for my stain.
Never believe, though in my nature reigned,
10 All frailties that besiege all kinds of blood,
That it could so preposterously be stained,
To leave for nothing all thy sum of good;
    For nothing this wide universe I call
    Save thou my Rose; in it thou art my all.

110

Alas, 'tis true, I have gone here and there
And made myself a motley to the view,
Gored mine own thoughts, sold cheap what is most dear,
Made old offences of affections new.
5 Most true it is that I have looked on truth
Askance and strangely. But, by all above,
These blenches gave my heart another youth,
And worse essays proved thee my best of love.
Now all is done, have what shall have no end;
10 Mine appetite I never more will grind
On newer proof to try an older friend,
A god in love, to whom I am confined.
    Then give me welcome, next my heaven the best,
    Even to thy pure and most most loving breast.

2   *guilty goddess* – his 'Muse', presumably having inspired him to write for the stage.

4   *public means* – earning his keep by writing and performing for the public, as opposed to private means or inherited wealth.

4   *public manners* – 'vulgar manners', such as those exhibited in the pit at the theatre.

5   *brand* – mark burned into the skin of a convicted criminal.

6–7 'From this cause, my gentler nature is almost entirely taken over by vulgar, theatrical, public manners'.

7   *the dyer's hand* – cloth dyers were identifiable by their coloured hands.

10 *eisel* – vinegar, popularly thought of as a cure for plague, and also known as a stain remover.

13 *Pity* – have sorrow for me, adapted as a **pun** (see page 182) in line 14.

14 *pity* – forgiveness, not the sorrow of line 13.

Do you agree that this whole sonnet is a piece of elaborate irony? Why (not)?

---

1   *impression fill* – filling or curing the mark of a branding-iron stamped into his forehead (see 111.5).

2   *vulgar scandal* – common rumour-mongers.

3   *o'er-green* – make innocent; 'cover with innocence'.

8   *steeled* – braced, fortified with steel.

8   *or changes right or wrong* – changes either what is right or what is wrong.

9   *abyss* – bottomless pit.

10 *adder's sense* – adders were commonly believed to be deaf.

12 *dispense* – get rid of.

13 *purpose* – endeavours, artistic achievement, or intentions.

111

O, for my sake do you with fortune chide,
The guilty goddess of my harmful deeds,
That did not better for my life provide
Than public means which public manners breeds.
5　Thence comes it that my name receives a brand,
And almost thence my nature is subdued
To what it works in, like the dyer's hand.
Pity me then, and wish I were renewed,
Whilst like a willing patient I will drink
10　Potions of eisel 'gainst my strong infection;
No bitterness that I will bitter think,
Nor double penance to correct correction.
　　Pity me then, dear friend, and I assure ye
　　Even that your pity is enough to cure me.

112

Your love and pity doth th'impression fill
Which vulgar scandal stamped upon my brow;
For what care I who calls me well or ill,
So you o'er-green my bad, my good allow?
5　You are my all the world, and I must strive
To know my shames and praises from your tongue –
None else to me, nor I to none alive,
That my steeled sense or changes, right or wrong.
In so profound abyss I throw all care
10　Of others' voices, that my adder's sense,
To critic and to flatterer stoppèd are.
Mark how with my neglect I do dispense:
　　You are so strongly in my purpose bred
　　That all the world besides, methinks, they're dead.

2   *governs me* – the eye, which gives the information necessary to walk round.

3   *part* – divide between imagining the lover and taking in objects in front of him.

4   *out* – 1) dark, like a light being out; 2) extinguished.

5   *form* – shape or image.

7   *quick objects* – living objects which fleetingly pass in front of the eyes.

8   The eye cannot retain images of which it catches sight.

13 *replete* – full up.

14 *makes mine eye untrue* – because all shapes become translated into images of the beloved, the mind can no longer distinguish a true picture of the beloved from another object translated to (his) image.

Why does the poet give so many examples of opposites in lines 9–12?

1   *crowned* – 1) ennobled; 2) blessed; 3) preoccupied.

2   *monarch's plague* – monarchs were especially susceptible to flatterers – hence their particular plague.

3   The philosophical basis of this sonnet is again the question of the Platonic shadow; whether the eye delivers truth to the mind, or whether the eye can trick the mind.

4   *alchemy* – love makes me see lead as gold.

6   *cherubins* – cherubim, the highest form of angels.

9   *'tis the first* – it is flattery, i.e. lines 1–2, not 3–4.

9   *in my seeing* – 1) 'in my view'; 2) my power of sight.

10–11 *most kingly drinks* – drinks the cup of flattery like a king who enjoys being flattered.

11 *what with his gust is 'greeing* – what is agreeable to his taste.

How does this sonnet elaborate the argument of Sonnet 113?

113

Since I left you mine eye is in my mind,
And that which governs me to go about
Doth part his function and is partly blind,
Seems seeing, but effectually is out;
5   For it no form delivers to the heart
Of bird, of flower, or shape which it doth latch,
Of his quick objects hath the mind no part,
Nor his own vision holds what it doth catch;
For if it see the rud'st or gentlest sight,
10 The most sweet favour or deformèd'st creature,
The mountain or the sea, the day, or night,
The crow, or dove, it shapes them to your feature.
    Incapable of more, replete with you,
    My most true mind thus makes mine eye untrue.

114

Or whether doth my mind, being crowned with you,
Drink up the monarch's plague, this flattery,
Or whether I shall say mine eye saith true,
And that your love taught it this alchemy,
5   To make of monsters and things indigest
Such cherubins as your sweet self resemble,
Creating every bad a perfect best
As fast as objects to his beams assemble?
O, 'tis the first, 'tis flatt'ry in my seeing,
10 And my great mind most kingly drinks it up,
Mine eye well knows what with his gust is 'greeing,
And to his palate doth prepare the cup.
    If it be poisoned, 'tis the lesser sin
    That mine eye loves it and doth first begin.

4 *flame* – love (see 109.2).

5 *reckoning* – counting, as in 'ticking'.

7 *Tan sacred beauty* – sacred beauty must be pure white, so any darkening at all makes it no longer pure (see 101.2–8).

7 *blunt the sharp'st intents* – see **Hamlet** 3.3:
'Though inclination be sharp as will,
My stronger guilt defeats my strong intent'
and 3.4: 'I come to whet thy almost blunted purpose'.

8 Again, see **Hamlet**.

12 *Crowning the present* – see 114.1.

13 *Love is a babe* – alluding to Cupid, cherub-god of love.

---

4 *remover* – one who moves away, who puts a distance in between.

5 *mark* – navigational reference point, used at sea.

7 *the star* – probably the Pole Star, marking north.

7 *wand'ring barque* – a barque is small ship; *wand'ring* suggests travelling all over the place, rather than being lost.

8 *worth's...height* – the sixteenth and early seventeenth centuries were the heyday of piracy, and a Spanish ship's worth was usually reckoned by the treasure in its hold. English ships were much smaller than the tall galleons of the Spanish. The sense is that the star guides great and lowly alike, without prejudice (see 80.8, 86.1,121.11).

12 *edge of doom* – the end of time, the day/sword of judgement.

13/14 *proved/loved* – single syllables.

> This sonnet has been read as praise of an absolute love which triumphs over time. It has also been read sceptically: love is so perfect it is impossible, and so no man ever loved.
> Which interpretation comes closest to yours and why?

115

Those lines that I before have writ do lie,
Even those that said I could not love you dearer;
Yet then my judgement knew no reason why
My most full flame should afterwards burn clearer.
5 But reckoning time, whose millioned accidents
Creep in 'twixt vows and change decrees of kings,
Tan sacred beauty, blunt the sharp'st intents,
Divert strong minds to th' course of alt'ring things –
Alas, why, fearing of time's tyranny,
10 Might I not then say 'Now I love you best',
When I was certain o'er incertainty,
Crowning the present, doubting of the rest?
    Love is a babe; then might I not say so,
    To give full growth to that which still doth grow.

116

Let me not to the marriage of true minds
Admit impediments. Love is not love
Which alters when it alteration finds,
Or bends with the remover to remove.
5 O no, it is an ever fixèd mark
That looks on tempests and is never shaken;
It is the star to every wand'ring barque,
Whose worth's unknown, although his height be taken.
Love's not time's fool, though rosy lips and cheeks
10 Within his bending sickle's compass come;
Love alters not with his brief hours and weeks,
But bears it out even to the edge of doom.
    If this be error and upon me proved,
    I never writ, nor no man ever loved.

1 *scanted* – stinted.

4 *bonds* – a seafaring as well as a legal term. His whole cargo belongs to the subject.

6 *given to time* – wasted.

7 *hoisted* – in nautical terms this distinctly means 'set out from harbour' as opposed to 'set sail', which may mean 'alter course'.
sail – presumably the sail of his saucy barque (80.7), i.e. his writing. Possibly a **pun** (see page 182) on 'sale', the poet having perhaps sold his 'dear-purchased' work elsewhere.

7 *winds* – long i – pronounced as a full rhyme with 'minds'.

9 *errors* – 1) mistakes; 2) sins; 3) in navigational terms 'to err' would be to stray from a prescribed course, hence the religious **metaphor** (see page 181) in 2).

9 *accumulate* – add up.

11 *level* – aim and range of fire of a gun – here, the subject's anger shown in (his) frown.

What kind of 'love' (line 3) is this sonnet about?

2 *eager compounds* – 'sharp sauce' or piquant appetisers.

4 *sicken* – deliberately make ourselves sick.

4 *purge* – remove from the stomach what is making the patient ill.

7 *meetness* – appropriateness, pleasure.

8 *diseased* – the metaphor is that he has taken another lover, for fear of something wrong in his relationship with the subject. **Pun** (see page 182) on *dis-ease*, unease.

11 *medicine* – the other lover, the purgative.

12 *rank* – smelling.

14 *Drugs poison him* – the affair with the other lover has backfired on the poet.

The phrase in line 14 'so fell sick of you' has two possible, and contrasting meanings. What are they and do you think the pun is intended?

117

Accuse me thus: that I have scanted all
Wherein I should your great deserts repay,
Forgot upon your dearest love to call
Whereto all bonds do tie me day by day.
5 That I have frequent been with unknown minds,
And given to time your own dear-purchased right;
That I have hoisted sail to all the winds
Which should transport me farthest from your sight.
Book both my wilfulness and errors down,
10 And on just proof surmise accumulate;
Bring me within the level of your frown,
But shoot not at me in your wakened hate,
　　Since my appeal says I did strive to prove
　　The constancy and virtue of your love.

118

Like as, to make our appetites more keen,
With eager compounds we our palate urge;
As to prevent our maladies unseen
We sicken to shun sickness when we purge:
5 Even so, being full of your ne'er cloying sweetness,
To bitter sauces did I frame my feeding,
And, sick of welfare, found a kind of meetness
To be diseased ere that there was true needing.
Thus policy in love, t'anticipate
10 The ills that were not, grew to faults assured,
And brought to medicine a healthful state
Which, rank of goodness, would by ill be cured.
　　But thence I learn, and find the lesson true:
　　Drugs poison him that so fell sick of you.

1 *siren* – creatures of Greek mythology, half bird, half woman, whose sweet singing voices tempted sailors to their doom. When Ulysses heard them he lashed himself to his mast while his sailors worked the ship with their ears stuffed full of wax.

2 *limbecks* – chemists' flasks, which used to be the main component of a still.

3 This parodies a sorcerer mixing a potion.

4 The parody is perhaps of a sorcerer becoming more and more heavily embroiled in his experiments and putting his soul in greater and greater danger.

7 His eyes have bulged out.

8 *distraction* – delirium.

10 There is a **pun** (see page 182) on 'still': 1) a person of excellence is made even better when cured with an 'evil still' (vile medicine); 2) excellent people are made even better by being touched with evil and still being able to rally.

---

13 *to my content* – accepting my rebuke.

3 *under my transgression bow* – bow his head in penitence in the hope of forgiveness for his sin (see note 12).

8 *weigh* – consider.

9 *remembered* – three syllables (re-mem-bred), not four.

10 *My deepest sense* – presumably his spiritual sense, in the way that spirit was an extra humour, the quintessence.

11 *tendered* – administered. Two syllables to make a full rhyme.

12 *salve* – ointment, a **metaphor** (see page 181) for a tendered apology.

12 *fits* – makes fit or well.

13 *trespass* – offence.

In lines 13–14, what is the fee and what is the ransom?

119

What potions have I drunk of siren tears
Distilled from limbecks foul as hell within,
Applying fears to hopes, and hopes to fears,
Still losing when I saw myself to win!
5 What wretched errors hath my heart committed,
Whilst it hath thought itself so blessèd never!
How have mine eyes out of their spheres been fitted
In the distraction of this madding fever!
O benefit of ill! Now I find true
10 That better is by evil still made better,
And ruined love when it is built anew
Grows fairer than at first, more strong, far greater.
So I return rebuked to my content,
And gain by ills thrice more than I have spent.

120

That you were once unkind befriends me now,
And for that sorrow which I then did feel
Needs must I under my transgression bow,
Unless my nerves were brass or hammered steel.
5 For if you were by my unkindness shaken
As I by yours, you've past a hell of time,
And I, a tyrant, have no leisure taken
To weigh how once I suffered in your crime.
O that our night of woe may be remembered
10 My deepest sense how hard true sorrow hits,
As soon to you as you to me then tendered
The humble salve which wounded bosoms fits!
But that your trespass now becomes a fee;
Mine ransoms yours, and yours must ransom me.

6   *sportive* – over-lustful (see 45.1, 63.3 and 67.3).

7   *frailer spies* – people who spy on him, who are just as sinful. Also literally 'weaker eyes'.

9   *level* – aim (see 117.10).

11   *straight...bevel* – the image is of a looker with his head leaning (bevelled) to one side, having the effect that a man standing straight seems to be leaning over. A carpenter's bevel is an instrument for measuring angle, used in ship-building; the 'seems bevel' effect would be important to seafarers taking an angle from a sextant in a heavy sea (see 116.8).

12   *must not* – ought not.

In lines 1–4 why is it better to be bad than simply to be thought bad?

1   *thy tables* – 1) your poems or poems about you; 2) your notebook.

2   *Full charactered* – engraved.

3   *idle rank* – rows of verse in the book.

6   *subsist* – exist, or be alive.

7   *Till each to razed oblivion* – until each character is erased forever (into oblivion).

7–8 *yield his part, Of thee* – give up the aspect he (each character) represents, into oblivion (death).

8   *thy record* – recollection of you, with a **pun** (see page 182) on 'your record of events'. Second syllable stressed.

8   *missed* – a **pun** (see page 182) on 'clouded in the mists of time'.

9   A sub-clause relating directly to line 14.

12   *those tables* – the 'tables of his heart' as in Sonnet 24.

12   *that receive thee more* – his heart still contains blank pages, unlike a completed book of sonnets.

13   *adjunct* – additional reminder.

14   *import* – imply.

121

'Tis better to be vile than vile esteemed,
When not to be receives reproach of being,
And the just pleasure lost, which is so deemed
Not by our feeling but by others' seeing.
5 For why should others' false adulterate eyes
Give salutation to my sportive blood?
Or on my frailties why are frailer spies,
Which in their wills count bad what I think good?
No, I am that I am, and they that level
10 At my abuses reckon up their own,
I may be straight, though they themselves be bevel;
By their rank thoughts, my deeds must not be shown,
    Unless the general evil they maintain:
    All men are bad and in their badness reign.

122

Thy gift, thy tables, are within my brain
Full charactered with lasting memory,
Which shall above that idle rank remain
Beyond all date, even to eternity;
5 Or at the least so long as brain and heart
Have faculty by nature to subsist,
Till each to razed oblivion yield his part
Of thee, thy record never can be missed:
That poor retention could not so much hold,
10 Nor need I tallies thy dear love to score;
Therefore to give them from me was I bold,
To trust those tables that receive thee more.
    To keep an adjunct to remember thee
    Were to import forgetfulness in me.

2 *pyramids* – a general term for ancient monuments.

3 *novel* – new.

3 *strange* – impressive, unusual.

5 *dates* – of birth and death.

7 *born* – a **pun** (see page 182) between the senses of 'carried', 'harvest produce' (bourn), 'given birth' and 'limit, boundary'.

9 *Thy registers...I both defy* – No written or physical records is absolutely true. That which was really seen by previous generations cannot be precisely preserved (see 108.1).

10 *wond'ring* – two syllables.

11 See note 9.

14 *thy scythe* – the destruction wrought by the passage of time.

Compare the ideas expressed in this sonnet with the ideas expressed in Sonnet 122.

---

1 *my dear love* – his precious emotion of love.

1 *child of state* – circumstance or fashion.

2 *for* – as.

2 *be unfathered* – disowned by its father (here the Friend).

3 *as* – since, because. If his love was just the product of circumstance or fashion it would be subject to the caprices of time and fortune.

5 It was built out of something quite other than the accidents of time.

6–7 *thrallèd* – to become enslaved or bonded. Discontent is therefore the slave/subject of time/fashion.

10 *leases of short numbered hours* – political satire, to suggest that policies lasted a matter of hours only.

11 *hugely politic* – extremely well-governed i.e. constant.

13–14 The poem finishes with the example of death-bed repentants who have been terrible wrong-doers all their lives, then, when impending death makes them scared of damnation, they change policy and disown their previous crimes.

123

No, time, thou shalt not boast that I do change!
Thy pyramids built up with newer might
To me are nothing novel, nothing strange,
They are but dressings of a former sight.
5 Our dates are brief, and therfore we admire
What thou dost foist upon us that is old,
And rather make them born to our desire
Than think that we before have heard them told.
Thy registers and thee I both defy,
10 Not wond'ring at the present nor the past;
For thy records and what we see doth lie,
Made more or less by thy continual haste.
    This I do vow, and this shall ever be:
    I will be true despite thy scythe and thee.

124

If my dear love were but the child of state,
It might for fortune's bastard be unfathered,
As subject to time's love or to time's hate,
Weeds among weeds or flowers with flowers gathered.
5 No, it was builded far from accident;
It suffers not in smiling pomp, nor falls
Under the blow of thrallèd discontent
Whereto th'inviting time our fashion calls.
It fears not policy, that heretic,
10 Which works on leases of short-numbered hours,
But all alone stands hugely politic,
That it nor grows with heat nor drowns with showers.
    To this I witness call the fools of time,
    Which die for goodness, who have lived for crime.

1	*Were't* – were it, if it were.
1	*canopy* – a covering, carried to protect the monarch's head from sun or rain. It was considered a great honour to be the canopy-bearer.
2	*extern* – face, appearance.
4	*Which* – i.e. eternity.
5	*form* – polite manners.
6	*and more* – what more is there to lose than 'all' except their lives?
6	*rent* – in return for the 'dwelling'.
7	*compound sweet* – sweet foods (see 118.2).
7	*simple savour* – ordinary food.
8	*gazing* – another reference to courtiers' privilege of being in the royal presence.
8	*spent* – finished, exhausted.
9	*obsequious* – respectful. Derived from mourners paying appropriate respects to a corpse.
10	*oblation* – holy offering.
13	*suborned* – bribed.
14	*When most impeached* – 1) when in most trouble; 2) when most people accused you.

> This irregular sonnet marks the end of the sequence of sonnets addressed to the Friend.

2	*glass* – mirror.
2	sickle-*hour* – hourglass.
4	*Thy lovers withering* – 1) all your lovers growing old; 2) your lovers withering away into age. His growing is equal to his lover's ageing (see 15.11).
5–8	The poet seems to flatter the young man that his continuing youthfulness makes time appear to stand still.
9	*minion* – minor courtier, male lover.
11	*audit* – account.
12	*quietus* – settlement of an account. 'Quietus est' would be written at the foot of an account ledger.

In the Quarto there are brackets to indicate the missing couplet.
The rhyme scheme in this poem is unusual. How would you divide it into units? Why to you think this poem has a different form? What dominant themes of the sequence do you find in this poem?

125

Were't aught to me I bore the canopy,
With my extern the outward honouring,
Or laid great bases for eternity
Which proves more short than waste or ruining?
5   Have I not seen dwellers on form and favour
Lose all and more by paying too much rent
For compound sweet forgoing simple savour,
Pitiful thrivers in their gazing spent?
No, let me be obsequious in thy heart,
10   And take thou my oblation, poor but free,
Which is not mixed with seconds, knows no art
But mutual render, only me for thee.
    Hence, thou suborned informer! A true soul
    When most impeached stands least in thy control.

126

O thou my lovely boy, who in thy power
Dost hold time's fickle glass, his sickle-hour;
Who hast by waning grown, and therein show'st,
Thy lovers withering, as thy sweet self grow'st –
5   If nature, sovereign mistress over wrack,
As thou goest onwards still will pluck thee back,
She keeps thee to this purpose: that her skill
May time disgrace, and wretched minutes kill.
Yet fear her, O thou minion of her pleasure!
10   She may detain, but not still keep her treasure.
    Her audit, though delayed, answered must be,
    And her quietus is to render thee.

This sonnet is the beginning of a new sequence of sonnets, mostly about the Dark Lady.

1   *fair* – beautiful (and blonde). There is a **pun** (see page 182) on 'fair' every time it appears in this sonnet.

4   *bastard shame* – the false beauty which is provided by make-up.

5   *each hand* – every individual's hand can usurp nature.

6   *foul* – ugly.

7   *bower* – bedchamber.

8   *profaned* – disrespect shown to a holy shrine.

9   *Therefore* – Therefore I can safely say…

10   *eyes so suited* – a **pun** (see page 182) on 'sooted'.

10   *At such* – to such who…

12   Make-up is a slander on God's creation.

13   *becoming* – 'fitting to their woe', with an equally important meaning of 'beautifying their woe'.

9–13   The lady's raven eyes are mourning for those who make themselves up to appear 'fair' (which she does not). Her eyes are so beautiful in their mourning that they convert people to her own type of beauty.

---

1   *my music* – a pet name, like 'my love'.

2–3   *sounds, With* – the music is perfectly united with her motion, another cause for his envy.

4   *wiry concord* – the instrument she plays is a 'virginal' which has a very wiry sound, more like a guitar, or lute, than a piano.

5   *jacks* – the jacks of a virginal are the upright pieces of wood which hold the quill. The whole key/jack/quill may have been popularly called a jack.

5   *nimble leap* – the virginal is played with the lid open and the sight of the jacks dancing to the music can be entrancing.

6   *tender inward* – the palm and underside of the fingers.

11   As the thumb was not used to play a keyboard, so the fingers crossed over one another. Therefore the image of walking would be more apt than for a modern pianist.

13   *happy* – blessed and joyful.

127

In the old age black was not counted fair,
Or if it were, it bore not beauty's name;
But now is black beauty's successive heir,
And beauty slandered with a bastard shame:
5   For since each hand hath put on nature's power,
Fairing the foul with art's false borrowed face,
Sweet beauty hath no name, no holy bower,
But is profaned, if not lives in disgrace.
Therefore my mistress' eyes are raven-black,
10 Her eyes so suited, and they mourners seem
At such who, not born fair, no beauty lack,
Sland'ring creation with a false esteem.
    Yet so they mourn, becoming of their woe,
    That every tongue says beauty should look so.

128

How oft, when thou, my music, music play'st,
Upon that blessèd wood whose motion sounds
With thy sweet fingers when thou gently sway'st,
The wiry concord that mine ear confounds,
5   Do I envy those jacks that nimble leap
To kiss the tender inward of thy hand
Whilst my poor lips, which should that harvest reap,
At the wood's boldness by thee blushing stand!
To be so tickled they would change their state
10 And situation with those dancing chips
O'er whom thy fingers walk with gentle gait,
Making dead wood more blessed than living lips.
    Since saucy jacks so happy are in this,
    Give them thy fingers, me thy lips to kiss.

1   *spirit* – 1) holy soul; 2) passion, the fiery blood-humour; 3) penis; 4) semen.

1–2 Lust (i.e. sex) by lavishing energy ('expense of spirit') in shameful extravagance; lust is satisfied by squandering the spirit in a void of guilt.

5   No sooner enjoyed than despised.

6   *Past reason hunted* – we lose all sense of reason when we pursue our lust.

6   *had* – in the sexual sense – see also *laid* and *taker* in line 8.

9   *Mad* – crazed in pursuit and a fool in possession.

11   *a bliss in proof* – wonderful while it is happening.

11   *and proved a very woe* – once tested, a complete disaster.

14   *heaven* – a clear **pun** (see page 182) on the female organ as a haven or harbour (see 110.13 and 137.6).

> How does 'a joy proposed; behind, a dream' in line 12 summarize the theme of the poem?

> The pace of this poem is rapid and frenetic. How does the poet achieve this pace?

---

3   *dun* – a dark brown colour.

5   *damasked* – a rich, deep pink colour (see 99.10).

11   *go* – walk; a goddess can presumably float or fly.

14   *belied* – falsely depicted.

> Compare the poet's description of a sexual relationship with a woman with his descriptions of his pure love for the Friend in earlier sonnets.

> See page 167 for a fuller exploration of this poem.

129

Th'expense of spirit in a waste of shame
Is lust in action; and till action, lust
Is perjured, murd'rous, bloody, full of blame,
Savage, extreme, rude, cruel, not to trust,
5 Enjoyed no sooner but despisèd straight,
Past reason hunted, and no sooner had
Past reason hated as a swallowed bait
On purpose laid to make the taker mad;
Mad in pursuit and in possession so,
10 Had, having, and in quest to have, extreme;
A bliss in proof and proved a very woe;
Before, a joy proposed; behind, a dream.
    All this the world well knows, yet none knows well
    To shun the heaven that leads men to this hell.

130

My mistress' eyes are nothing like the sun;
Coral is far more red than her lips' red.
If snow be white, why then her breasts are dun;
If hairs be wires, black wires grow on her head.
5 I have seen roses damasked, red and white,
But no such roses see I in her cheeks;
And in some perfumes is there more delight
Than in the breath that from my mistress reeks.
I love to hear her speak, yet well I know,
10 That music hath a far more pleasing sound.
I grant I never saw a goddess go:
My mistress when she walks treads on the ground.
    And yet, be heaven, I think my love as rare
    As any she belied with false compare.

1   *so as thou art* – just as you are.

5   *in good faith* – in truth. It is a mild oath.

7   Why may he not be so bold as to say 'they err'? What power or influence do they have over him?

8   *swear* – linking back to 'in good faith' in line 5.

11   *One on another's neck* – one straight after the other in quick succession (proverbial).

14   *this slander* – i.e. line 6.

> *Does 'Thy black' in line 12 relate to 'thy face' in line 10? If so, does this contradict the implication in Sonnet 127 that the Lady has only dark eyes, not a dark skin?*

---

1   *as* – as though.

4   *ruth* – pity, compassion.

5   *sun of heaven* – 1) the sun, often compared to an eye; 2) an **allusion** (see page 179) to Christ.

7   *full star* – Venus, the 'evening star'.

7   *even* – evening. Two syllables, rhyming with *heaven*.

10   *beseem* – make your heart seem, or appear, this way.

11   *doth thee grace* – suits you, looks good on you.

12   *suit* – make it (your pity) the same. Also a **pun** (see page 182) on *soot*, darken your pity.

14   *foul* – ugly.

14   *complexion* – disposition, as well as complexion.

> *In Sonnet 131 the poet says he would 'not be so bold' as to state publicly how beautiful he finds his mistress. In Sonnet 132 he says 'Then will I swear beauty herself is black'. Why would he change his mind? What is the poet asking of his mistress in this poem?*

131

Thou art as tyrannous so as thou art
As those whose beauties proudly make them cruel,
For well thou know'st to my dear doting heart
Thou art the fairest and most precious jewel.
5   Yet, in good faith, some say that thee behold
Thy face hath not the power to make love groan.
To say they err I dare not be so bold,
Although I swear it to my self alone;
And, to be sure that is not false I swear,
10 A thousand groans but thinking on thy face
One on another's neck do witness bear
Thy black is fairest in my judgement's place.
     In nothing art thou black save in thy deeds,
     And thence this slander, as I think, proceeds.

132

Thine eyes I love, and they as pitying me –
Knowing thy heart torment me with disdain –
Have put on black, and loving mourners be,
Looking with pretty ruth upon my pain;
5   And truly not the morning sun of heaven
Better becomes the gray cheeks of the east,
Nor that full star that ushers in the even
Doth half that glory to the sober west,
As those two mourning eyes become thy face.
10 O, let it then as well beseem thy heart
To mourn for me, since mourning doth thee grace,
And suit thy pity like in every part.
     Then will I swear beauty herself is black,
     And all they foul that thy complexion lack.

1	*Beshrew* – cursed be...
2	*deep wound* – 1) heart-sickness; 2 female sexual organs.
4	*slave to slavery* – 1) because the Friend is slave to another slave; 2) she is slavery personified.
5	*Me from myself* – 1) her cruel eye has distracted him; 2) she distracts his 'true self' and made him unfaithful.
5	*thy cruel eye* – the colour of her eye, yet 'eye' could mean her sexual organs, given to the friend.
6	*next self* – next dearest self, presumably his friend, so close a friend as to be virtually another self.
6	*harder hast engrossed* – a double-entendre.
8	Tormented three times – crossed three times, not crossed 27 times!
8	*crossed* – cheated, hence modern 'double-crossed'.
9	*steel bosom's ward* – cell, hence 'prison warders' (see Sonnet 48).
11	*keeps me* – imprisons me in a keep. Also **puns** (see page 182) on 'retains me' and 'provides for me'.
13	*pent in thee* – imprisoned in her, with double meaning.

2	*mortgaged* – literally 'engaged until death'. *Will* – a **pun** (see page 182) on William, sexual desire, penis.
3	*forfeit* – ransom (see Sonnet 107).
3	*that other mine* – his next self.
4	*restore* – return.
4	*to be my comfort still* – from Psalm 23.
5	*thou wilt not* – 1) will not; 2) desire it not; the same ambiguity applies to what he 'will not'.
6–7	*covetous* – envious.
7	*surety-like* – to stand surety is to guarantee a lender will pay back what is loaned.
9	*statute* – terms of the bond.
10	*usurer* – one who lends money at interest (see 4.7). If a usurer puts all his money 'out to use', it can all earn interest. She puts all herself to sexual use.
11	*sue* – claim.
11	*came debtor* – became a debtor.

How does the phrase 'pays the whole' in line 14 link back to line 10?

Compare Sonnets 133 and 134 with Sonnets 40–42.

133

Beshrew that heart that makes my heart to groan
For that deep wound it gives my friend and me!
Is't not enough to torture me alone,
But slave to slavery my sweet'st friend must be?
5 Me from myself thy cruel eye hath taken,
And my next self thou harder hast engrossed,
Of him, myself, and thee I am forsaken –
A torment thrice threefold thus to be crossed.
Prison my heart in thy steel bosom's ward,
10 But then my friend's heart let my poor heart bail;
Whoe'er keeps me, let my heart be his guard;
Thou canst not then use rigour in my jail.
    And yet thou wilt; for I being pent in thee,
    Perforce am thine, and all that is in me.

134

So, now I have confessed that he is thine,
And I myself am mortgaged to thy will,
Myself I'll forfeit, so that other mine
Thou wilt restore to be my comfort still.
5 But thou wilt not, nor he will not be free,
For thou art covetous, and he is kind.
He learned but surety-like to write to me
Under that bond that him as fast doth bind.
The statute of thy beauty thou wilt take,
10 Thou usurer that put'st forth all to use,
And sue a friend came debtor for my sake;
So him I lose through my unkind abuse.
    Him have I lost; thou hast both him and me;
    He pays the whole, and yet am I not free.

I   *Will* – this poem revolves around the multiple **puns** (see page 182) of this
     name. The italics show italics in Quarto: (i) desire – want/intention; (ii)
     desire – lust; (iii) the male organ; (iv) the female organ; (v) willing,
     prepared to; (vi) William, the name.

3   *vex* – annoy, here probably meaning 'pursue'.

4   *addition* – recommendation or addition of his part to hers.

5   *Wilt* – 1) desire; 2) weaken – wilt in her resolve.

6   *vouchsafe* – agree.

8   *fair acceptance* – sexual favour or friendship by women.

9   *The sea* – see 110.13, 129.14 and 137.6 for other references to female
     parts as aspects of the sea.

13   *unkind* – cruel, being a reference here to his friend's disloyalty.

13   *fair beseechers* – his friend, but with insincerity, as we say 'fair-weather
     friends'.

13   *kill* – 1) the friend, 'killing' the poet with unkindness; 2) score a sexual 'hit' –
     the word 'die' meant sexual climax.

> *Using the line 1 note, examine the seven italicized 'Wills' in the sonnet.*
> *What message do the puns convey?*

I   *soul* – inward spirit; on one level the poem is about conscience checking
     lustful, immoral behaviour.

4–5 *fulfil* – 1) satisfy, in line 5, gains another, punning sense; 2) fully fill.

5   *treasure* – 1) worth; 2) female sexual organ (see 20.14).

9   *untold* – uncounted, i.e. unnoticed.

10   *store's* – 1) total's; 2) sexual organ's.

11   *nothing hold me* – he is true, not *held* by any other woman, but he has
     something, sweet she might hold, perhaps?

13   *Take but my name* – presumably, just take my 'will'.

13   *still* – 1) anyway; 2) calm, to make it 'still', or dead, a double-entendre.

135

Whoever hath her wish, thou hast thy *Will*,
And *Will* to boot, and *Will* in overplus,
More than enough am I that vex thee still,
To thy sweet will making addition thus.
5   Wilt thou, whose will is large and spacious,
Not once vouchsafe to hide my will in thine?
Shall will in others seem right gracious,
And in my will no fair acceptance shine?
The sea, all water, yet receives rain still,
10   And in abundance addeth to his store;
So thou, being rich in *Will*, add to thy *Will*,
One will of mine to make thy large *Will* more.
      Let no unkind no fair beseechers kill;
      Think all but one, and me in that one *Will*.

136

If thy soul check thee that I come so near,
Swear to thy blind soul that I was thy *Will*,
And will, thy soul knows, is admitted there;
Thus far for love, my love-suit, sweet, fulfil.
5   *Will* will fulfill the treasure of thy love,
Ay, fill it full with *wills* and my will one.
In things of great receipt with ease we prove,
Among a number one is reckoned none.
Then in the number let me pass untold,
10   Though in thy store's account I one must be;
For nothing hold me, so it please thee hold
That nothing me a something, sweet, to thee.
      Take but my name thy love, and love that still,
      And then thou lov'st me for my name is Will.

1   *blind fool love* – an allusion to Cupid, and perhaps to the blind eyes of Sonnet 136.

2   *not what they see* – meaning 'report not what they know' (see Sonnets 113, 127, 131 and 132).

3   *where it lies* – who or what possesses it (beauty).

6   *ride* – 1) a boat rides the tide in a harbour as it rises and falls; 2) bawdy innuendo.

8   *tied* – 1) tied, linked; 2) Quarto has 'tide' because the heart moves with the tide of the eye.

9   *several plot* – a plot of land shared by several gardeners, possibly with bawdy overtones of 'ploughing'.

10 *common place* – 1) well-known saying; 2) a common, or shared piece of ground (place).

12 *foul* – dark-skinned, possibly intending 'ugly'.

Compare this with Sonnet 113.

---

9   *wherefore* – why.

11 *habit* – 1) clothing; 2) custom.

11 *seeming trust* – love looks best when dressed in apparent trust, i.e. the best relationship is one in which both appear to trust the other, even if they know the trust to be false.

12 *told* – counted up.

13 *lie* – 1) tell lies; 2) have sex with.

14 *we flattered be* – we flatter ourselves – I that I am young, she that she is truthful.

How does the poet excuse her falsehood in lines 7–8?

What is the poet's 'fault'?

137

Thou blind fool love, what dost thou to mine eyes
That they behold and see not what they see?
They know what beauty is, see where it lies,
Yet what the best is take the worst to be.
5   If eyes corrupt by over-partial looks,
Be anchored in the bay where all men ride,
Why of eyes' falsehood hast thou forgèd hooks,
Whereto the judgement of thy heart is tied?
Why should my heart think that a several plot
10   Which my heart knows the wide world's common place? –
Or mine eyes, seeing this, say this is not,
To put fair truth upon so foul a face?
    In things right true my heart and eye have erred,
    And to this false plague are they now transferred.

138

When my love swears that she is made of truth
I do believe her though I know she lies,
That she might think me some untutored youth,
Unlearnèd in the world's false subtleties.
5   Thus vainly thinking that she thinks me young,
Although she knows my days are past the best,
Simply I credit her false-speaking tongue,
On both sides thus is simple truth suppressed:
But wherefore says she not she is unjust,
10   And wherefore say not I that I am old?
O, love's best habit is in seeming trust,
And age in love love's not to have years told.
    Therefore I lie with her, and she with me,
    And in our faults by lies we flattered be.

1   *call not me* – as a witness.

1   *justify* – defend, condone.

3   *Wound me not with thine eye* – do not wound me by looking at others.

4   *Use power with power* – use power powerfully.

4   *slay* – kill.

4   *by Art* – by deception, artfulness.

6   *forbear* – please do not.

6   *cunning* – the 'art' of line 4.

6   *thy might* – power of the truth, her willingness to leave him.

8   *o'erpressed* – over-run.

8   *bide* – manage.

9   *Let me excuse me* – 1) let me take my leave; 2) let me excuse myself in the following words 'ah…injuries'.

10   *pretty looks* – her enticing glances.

10   *mine enemies* – his downfall because he always gives in to them.

14   *Kill me outright with looks* – either look at me and therefore seduce me so I can forget my pain, or carry on avoiding me as you are and I will soon be finished off.

Although the poet says 'call not me to justify the wrong' does he begin to make excuses for the lady in the sestet?

Does the couplet surprise you with its violence?

---

1   *Be wise* – 'Be as wise…'.

1   *press* – antagonize. This seems to pick up the 'defences' of Sonnet 139.

2   *disdain* – the guilty looks and turning away of Sonnet 139 have become a proud and unkind haughtiness.

4   *The manner* – 1) in the tone of…; 2) the nature of.

4   *pity-wanting pain* 1) wanting to pain you; 2) 'my pain is pity-seeking'.

5   *wit* – wisdom, good sense.

5   *were* – full rhyme with 'near'.

7   *testy* – grumpy. Because they are so grumpy, their physicians are too scared to tell them the truth.

8–12   Despair will make me speak ill of you and the gossips will believe and magnify my malicious words.

13–14   So that I neither despair nor spread lies about you, please look me straight in the eye, though your heart may be elsewhere.

What is the poet asking of his mistress in this poem?

139

O call not me to justify the wrong
That thy unkindness lays upon my heart.
Wound me not with thine eye but with thy tongue;
Use power with power, and slay me not by art.
5   Tell me thou lov'st elsewhere, but in my sight,
Dear heart, forbear to glance thine eye aside.
What need'st thou wound with cunning when thy might
Is more than my o'erpressed defence can bide?
Let me excuse thee: 'Ah my love well knows,
10 Her pretty looks have been mine enemies,
And therefore from my face she turns my foes
That they elsewhere might dart their injuries.'
       Yet do not so; but since I am near slain,
       Kill me outright with looks, and rid my pain.

140

Be wise as thou art cruel, do not press
My tongue-tied patience with too much disdain,
Lest sorrow lend me words, and words express
The manner of my pity-wanting pain.
5   If I might teach thee wit, better it were
Though not to love, yet, love, to tell me so –
As testy sick men when their deaths be near
No news but health from their physicians know.
For if I should despair I should grow mad,
10 And in my madness might speak ill of thee.
Now this ill-wresting world is grown so bad
Mad slanders by mad ears believèd be.
       That I may not be so, nor thou belied,
       Bear thine eyes straight, though thy proud heart go wide.

2 *errors* – features thought not perfect.

3 *what they despise* – what his eyes find distasteful, or rather what his culture has taught his eyes to find displeasing.

5 *ears* – I find your voice less than pleasing.

6 *tender feeling* – the discriminating sense of touch; 'base touches' is a bawdy **pun** (see page 182).

11 *unswayed* – unconverted.

11 *the likeness of a man* – the mere shadow/picture, a hollow shell lacking his five senses.

12 *vassal-wretch* – serf, bondman. A medieval peasant belonged to the lord of the manor.

13–14 I consider my mistress or my fever of love ('my plague') to be my gain only to this extent: she makes me sin and inflicts pain on me.

What is the conflict within the poet about his feelings for his mistress?

Why do you think the poet considers sin and pain a gain? (Look at the first line of Sonnet 142.)

---

2 *Hate of my sin* – The lady's virtue turns out to be hatred of the poet's 'sin' which is his love for her.

2 *grounded on sinful loving* – 1) born out of his illicit love for her; 2) because she sinfully loves so many other men better. A brilliant ambiguity.

4 *it merits not reproving* – you're in no position to judge.

6 *prophaned* – see 127.8.

7 *false bonds* – see 134.8.

8 *revenues* – stressed on second syllable.

11–12 Become a compassionate person so that you yourself may deserve compassion.

13 *What thou dost hide* – i.e. pity

14 *By self example* – according to your own precedent.

141

In faith, I do not love thee with mine eyes,
For they in thee a thousand errors note;
But 'tis my heart that loves what they despise,
Who in despite of view is pleased to dote.
5   Nor are mine ears with thy tongue's tune delighted,
Nor tender feeling to base touches prone;
Nor taste, nor smell, desire to be invited
To any sensual feast with thee alone;
But my five wits nor my five senses can
10   Dissuade one foolish heart from serving thee,
Who leaves unswayed the likeness of a man,
Thy proud heart's slave and vassal-wretch to be.
     Only my plague thus far I count my gain:
     That she that makes me sin awards me pain.

142

Love is my sin, and thy dear virtue hate,
Hate of my sin, grounded on sinful loving.
O, but with mine compare thou thine own state,
And thou shalt find it merits not reproving;
5   Or if it do, not from those lips of thine
That have prophaned their scarlet ornaments
And sealed false bonds of love as oft as mine,
Robbed others' beds' revenues of their rents.
Be it lawful I love thee as thou lov'st those
10   Whom thine eyes woo as mine importune thee,
Root pity in thy heart, that when it grows
Thy pity may deserve to pitied be.
     If thou dost seek to have what thou dost hide,
     By self example mayst thou be denied.

2   an escaped chicken.

3   *all swift dispatch* – every effort.

4   *pursuit* – emphasis must be on first syllable.

5   *holds her in chase* – chases after her.

6–7 Cries and follows her.

8   *Not prizing* – neither caring nor noticing.

13   *Will* – see Sonnets 135 and 136.

14   *still* – calm (see 136.13 for innuendo).

Does this rural, domestic picture suggest the mistress views the poet's love for her as rather pathetic?

---

1   *comfort* – One love gives comfort, the other leads him into despair. Both 'comfort' and 'despair' have strong religious/spiritual connotations.

2   *two spirits* – ghosts.

2   *suggest* – tempt, haunt.

9   *fiend* – demon.

10   *yet not directly tell* – but cannot be sure.

12   !) 'I presume one angel is making the other miserable' extends the idea of suffering in line 5; 2) The good angel is stuck in the bad one's vagina.

14   1) Until my mistress stops seeing my friend. 2) Also suggests that the good angel needs to be smoked out of the bad angel's vagina (picking up the 'hell' as intercourse pun from line 12). 3) 'fire...out' could also refer to venereal disease: till my bad angel gives my good one disease ('fire').

What two meanings can be given to 'being both from me, both to each friend' in line 11?

143

Lo, as a care-full housewife runs to catch
One of her feathered creatures broke away,
Sets down her babe and makes all swift dispatch
In pursuit of the thing she would have stay,
5   Whilst her neglected child holds her in chase,
Cries to catch her whose busy care is bent
To follow that which flies before her face,
Not prizing her poor infant's discontent:
So runn'st thou after that which flies from thee,
10 Whilst I, thy babe, chase thee afar behind;
But if thou catch thy hope, turn back to me
And play the mother's part: kiss me, be kind.
    So will I pray that thou mayst have thy Will,
    If thou turn back and my loud crying still.

144

Two loves I have of comfort and despair,
Which like two spirits do suggest me still.
The better angel is a man right fair,
The worser spirit a woman coloured ill.
5   To win me soon to hell my female evil
Tempteth my better angel from my side,
And would corrupt my saint to be a devil,
Wooing his purity with her foul pride.
And whether that my angel be turned fiend,
10 Suspect I may, yet not directly tell;
But being both from me, both to each friend,
I guess one angel in another's hell.
    Yet this shall I ne'er know, but live in doubt
    Till my bad angel fire my good one out.

3   *languished* – suffered, pined away.

8   *anew* – once again. She was not cruel before.
9   *end* – an ending, that is a 'd', which makes the present tense into past, and thereby ended her hatred.

13 *hate away* – 'hat away', a possible reference to Shakespeare's wife, Anne Hathaway.
14 *And saved* – It has been suggested that this, when spoken aloud, sounds like 'Anne saved' because the 'd' in 'and' was rarely pronounced.

---

1   *sinful earth* – the 'earth' is the body; the soul lies at the centre of the body, giving it stability.
2   *My sinful earth* – the phrase from line 1 may be accidentally repeated. The clearest evidence for this is that the line now has six stresses, and is the only hexameter in the Quarto. Editors have often inserted their own guess at what Shakespeare may have intended here.
4   *costly gay* – expensively fine or colourful.
5   *lease* – lifespan.
6   *thy fading mansion* – the body and a contrast with the biblical mansions of heaven.
10 *pine* – waste away.
10 *aggravate* – accumulate.
11 *Buy terms divine* – purchase unlimited time in heaven.
11 *in selling hours of dross* – by foregoing opportunities to indulge the body in trivial things.
13–14 By depriving the body, the 'soul' is depriving death, which feeds upon the body; this death will be starved and die, and the soul will enjoy immortality.

How are the body and soul interdependent according to this poem?

145

Those lips that love's own hand did make,
Breathed forth that sound that said 'I hate'
To me that languished for her sake;
But when she saw my woeful state,
5   Straight in her heart did mercy come,
Chiding that tongue that ever sweet,
Was used in giving gentle doom,
And taught it thus anew to greet:
'I hate' she altered with an end
10   That followed it as gentle day
Doth follow night who, like a fiend,
From heaven to hell is flown away.
        'I hate' from hate away she threw,
        And saved my life, saying 'not you'.

146

Poor soul, the centre of my sinful earth,
My sinful earth these rebel powers that thee array;
Why dost thou pine within and suffer dearth,
Painting thy outward walls so costly gay?
5   Why so large cost, having so short a lease,
Dost thou upon thy fading mansion spend?
Shall worms, inheritors of this excess,
Eat up thy charge? Is this thy body's end?
Then, soul, live thou upon thy servant's loss,
10   And let that pine to aggravate thy store.
Buy terms divine in selling hours of dross;
Within be fed, without be rich no more.
        So shalt thou feed on death, that feeds on men,
        And death once dead, there's no more dying then.

5   *reason* – sanity, ability to think clearly.
5   *physician to my love* – doctor trying to cure me of an unwise love.
7   *approve* – believe.
8   *which physic did except* – which the medical profession took exception to.
10 *evermore* – If 'mad' means made, it would be 'increasing unrest' (disquiet); if 'mad' means mad, it would be 'unrest for ever more'.
13 *fair* – beautiful.
13 *bright* – holy, resplendent, angelic.
14 *black* – wicked.
14 *dark* – treacherous.

What two different senses are there if we put a comma in line 12 after either 'random' or 'truth'?

Compare this sonnet with 118–19. What common concerns are there?

---

2   1) are not at all like eyes which see properly; 2) do not see what is really there to be seen (i.e. are blind to reality).
4   *censures* – criticizes, scolds.
7   *denote* – represent.
10 *vexed* – tired, painful, aching.
12 *The sun itself sees not* – The Quarto has 'it self'. 'Self' can be compounded both with 'it', 'itself', and, in a secondary sense, 'sees', 'selfsees'. The Elizabethans believed the eye emitted beams of light, as well as perceiving, taking in the world outside, therefore, when 'region clouds' hide the light, the sun cannot see and its vision of everything is changed.

14 *thy* – here he means the Dark Lady, whereas in line 13 'thou' refers to love personified (see **personification**, page 182).

Compare this sonnet with the theme of Sonnets 113–14. What do these sonnets say about love and distortion?

147

My love is a fever, longing still,
For that which longer nurseth the disease,
Feeding on that which doth preserve the ill,
Th'uncertain sickly appetite to please.
5 My reason, the physician to my love,
Angry that his prescriptions are not kept,
Hath left me, and I desperate now approve
Desire is death, which physic did except.
Past cure I am, now reason is past care,
10 And frantic mad with evermore unrest.
My thoughts and my discourse as madmen's are,
At random from the truth vainly expressed;
 For I have sworn thee fair, and thought thee bright,
 Who art as black as hell, as dark as night.

148

O me, what eyes hath love put in my head,
Which have no correspondence with true sight!
Or if they have, where is my judgement fled,
That censures falsely what they see aright?
5 If that be fair whereon my false eyes dote,
What means the world to say it is not so?
If it be not, then love doth well denote
Love's eye is not so true as all men's. No,
How can it, O, how can love's eye be true,
10 That is so vexed with watching and with tears?
No marvel then though I mistake my view,
The sun itself sees not, till heaven clears.
 O cunning love, with tears thou keep'st me blind
 Lest eyes, well seeing, thy foul faults should find!

2   *When against* – 'When I against...'.

2   *partake* – take sides.

3   *when I forgot* – when I, my self forgotten, Am...

1–4   One possible interpretation is 'How can you say I don't love you when I forget my "ego" and am a tyrant to myself – O, you cruel thing, you!' Another interpretation of line 3 is 'when I have gone so far as to forget even myself'.

7   *lour'st* – grimaces menacingly.

9   *in myself respect* – the same problem as at 148.12: self can couple with 'my', giving 'myself respect' or with 'respect', giving 'my self-respect'.

10   *thy service* – being her lover.

11   *thy defect* – her colour.

13   *But, love, hate on* – But, my love, continue to hate me.

13   *now I know thy mind* – 1) now I know what kind of person you are; 2) now I know how you feel about me.

14   The lady loves those who see her but the poet is blinded by love.

---

4   *becoming of* – making of...

5   *refuse* – rubbish, the very worst aspects of her deeds.

7   *warrantise* – guarantee.

8   *best* – good.

12   *my state* – a rare reference to Shakespeare's status but what does he mean by it – 'poor player', 'humble poet', 'commoner'?

13   *raised love* – a double-entendre.

149

Canst thou, O cruel, say I love thee not
When I against myself with thee partake:
Do I not think on thee when I forgot
Am of myself, all-tyrant for thy sake?
5 Who hateth thee that I do call my friend?
On whom frown'st thou that I do fawn upon?
Nay if thou lour'st on me do I not spend
Revenge upon myself with present moan?
What merit do I in my self respect
10 That is so proud thy service to despise,
When all my best doth worship thy defect,
Commanded by the motion of thine eyes?
    But, love, hate on; for now I know thy mind.
    Those that can see thou lov'st, and I am blind.

150

O, from what power hast thou this powerful might
With insufficiency my heart to sway,
To make me give the lie to my true sight
And swear that brightness doth not grace the day?
5 Whence hast thou this becoming of things ill,
That in the very refuse of thy deeds
There is such strength and warrantise of skill
That in my mind thy worst all best exceeds?
Who taught thee how to make me love thee more
10 The more I hear and see just cause of hate?
O, though I love what others do abhor,
With others thou shouldst not abhor my state.
    If thy unworthiness raised love in me,
    More worthy I to be beloved of thee.

1   *Love is too young* – 'Love' is Cupid, the boy-god of love.
2   *born* – 1) born or conceived out of the act of love; 2) a burden carried by love.

6   *My nobler part* – his soul.

8   *Triumph in love* – either 'may triumph...' or 'A triumph in love, flesh,..'
8   *says no farther reason* – 1) puts up with no more argument from reason; 2) remains firm no longer than my reason.
9   An obvious innuendo.
11   *drudge* – menial servant.
14   *fall* – whilst obviously sexual, there is also an echo of the fall of Adam.

> *What does the poet mean by 'gross body's treason' (line 6)?*

---

2   *am forsworn* – break faith (with another lover, perhaps the 'Friend').
2   *twice forsworn* – she breaks two vows.
3   *bed-vow* – either a marriage vow, a common-law vow or a lover's oath.
2–4 Either you are false to your previous lover in sleeping with me or you are false to me in vowing hate after having vowed love.
7   *misuse* – 'use' her for 'immoral sex'.
8   An ambiguity allowed by the original punctuation: has he lost his 'faith in her' or has he lost his honest religious faith because of his relationship, making 'in thee' a clever innuendo?
9   *deep oaths* – 1) fast-binding oaths; 2) perhaps suggesting oaths sworn 'when deep in drink'.
9   *deep kindness* – a double-entendre, depending on the sexual meaning of 'kind' as in 134.6 and 12.
11   *enlighten thee* – make her seem fairer, or better, but not to make her better informed!
13   *perjured eye* – the eye lies on oath.

> *What might be the purpose, for the poet, of this sonnet?*

151

Love is too young to know what conscience is,
Yet who knows not conscience is born of love,
Then, gentle cheater, urge not my amiss,
Lest guilty of my faults thy sweet self prove.
5   For, thou betraying me, I do betray
My nobler part to my gross body's treason.
My soul doth tell my body that he may
Triumph in love; flesh stays no farther reason,
But rising at thy name doth point out thee
10   As his triumphant prize. Proud of this pride,
He is contented thy poor drudge to be,
To stand in thy affairs, fall by thy side.
      No want of conscience hold it that I call
      Her 'love' for whose dear love I rise and fall.

152

In loving thee thou know'st I am forsworn,
But thou art twice forsworn to me love swearing:
In act thy bed-vow broke, and new faith torn
In vowing new hate after new love bearing.
5   But why of two oaths' breach do I accuse thee
When I break twenty? I am perjured most,
For all my vows are oaths but to misuse thee,
And all my honest faith in thee is lost.
For I have sworn deep oaths of thy deep kindness,
10   Oaths of thy love, thy truth, thy constancy,
And to enlighten thee gave eyes to blindness,
Or made them swear against the thing they see.
      For I have sworn thee fair – more perjured eye,
      To swear against the truth so foul a lie.

1   *Cupid* – the love-god cherub who fired burning arrows, or *brands* into the hearts of those he made to fall in love.

2   *Dian's* – Roman goddess of hunting and chastity, associated with the moon.

3   *steep* – plunge, quench.

4   *valley-fountain* – a natural spring; that holy ground, where the gods lived.

6   *lively* – 1) living; 2) life-giving.

7   *seething bath* – hot spring, a spa with healing properties.

11 *withal* – 1) by now; 2) with all the brand's effects.

12 *hied* – travelled.

13 *sad distempered* – love-sick.

14 Cupid has re-kindled his arrows from the passion of her eyes.

---

3   *nymphs* – female immortals, ever youthful.

4   *tripping* – dancing, skipping.

5   *votary* – follower or server of a god or goddess, in this case, Diana.

7   *general* – Cupid.

7   *hot desire* – love, with a distinctly bawdy overtone.

8   *virgin hand disarmed* – possibly a bawdy innuendo.

9   *by* – nearby.

10 *heat perpetual* – everlasting heat.

11 Creating a health spa.

12 *I my mistress' thrall* – I my mistress's slave or vassal.

14 Possibly an obscure double-entendre.

How would you contrast Sonnets 153 and 154?

153

Cupid laid by his brand and fell asleep.
A maid of Dian's this advantage found,
And his love-kindling fire did quickly steep
In a cold valley-fountain of that holy ground,
5 Which borrowed from this holy fire of love
A dateless lively heat, still to endure,
And grew a seething bath which yet men prove
Against strong maladies a sovereign cure.
But at my mistress' eye love's brand new fired,
10 The boy for trial needs would touch my breast.
I, sick withal, the help of bath desired,
And thither hied, a sad distempered guest.
    But found no cure; the bath for my help lies
    Where Cupid got new fire: my mistress' eyes.

154

The little love-god lying once asleep
Laid by his side his heart-inflaming brand,
Whilst many nymphs that vowed chaste life to keep
Came tripping by; but in her maiden hand
5 The fairest votary took up that fire
Which many legions of true hearts had warmed,
And so the general of hot desire
Was sleeping by a virgin hand disarmed.
This brand she quenchèd in a cool well by,
10 Which from love's fire took heat perpetual,
Growing a bath and healthful remedy,
For men diseased; but I my mistress' thrall,
    Came there for cure; and this by that I prove:
    Love's fire heats water, water cools not love.

SHAKESPEARE'S LIFE
AND TIMES

We have very few certain facts about Shakespeare's life. He was born and baptized in Stratford-upon-Avon in 1564. He married Anne Hathaway in November 1582; his daughter Susanna was christened in May 1583, his twins, Hamnet and Judith, in 1585. In 1588 he is mentioned in a Stratford property law suit and in 1592 we know he was an actor and playwright in London, causing something of a stir as a 'Shakescene' and an 'upstart crow' according to the old playwright Robert Greene. From then on his history is told by the publication of his work, his continuous association with the acting company 'The Lord Chamberlain's Men', his purchase of increasingly large properties and a few odd legal matters.

The London he would have known was a city of great political importance, thriving trade and incredible culture. The 1590s were the later years of Queen Elizabeth I, the Spanish Armada had been defeated in 1588 and the Port of London was the trade capital of Northern Europe. There was peace of a kind and trade with all nations, including those around the Mediterranean, and there is a strong possibility that Shakespeare himself had been to sea in the 1580s, visiting Italy, France and Spain. Even if he had not, his chosen place of work, the Bankside of the Thames, would have had people of all nations visiting. Big theatre buildings were a new feature; they quickly established names still known today – The Swan, The Rose and The Globe. A whole district grew with them, providing entertainment for Londoners and visitors alike with taverns, bear gardens, cockpits, brothels. The theatres were on the south side of the river in the 1590s and they drew their operatives from the dockyard, shorebound sailors who turned their sailmaking and rigging skills to other uses.– building the scenery. This is why, even today, backstage terms are sailing jargon. This is possibly how Shakespeare himself found his way into the theatre world: back from a voyage, joining the theatre, turning his hand to acting, having a better idea for a play, writing it down.

And, being on the south side of the river, the theatres were close enough to draw the rich and privileged from the Court, yet far enough away for them to enjoy the play then disappear into the warren of back alleys and pubs, taverns and brothels. This way, the theatre slowly became fashionable and established as a meeting place for the very rich and the highest in society, who had previously remained at Court. It is possible that here Shakespeare became known to important and influential people; he came to know about political intrigues such as the trial of Dr Lopez, the Queen's Jewish physician, executed for spying in 1594, or the ill-fated Essex Rebellion of 1601 and the execution of the Earl of Essex himself.

With such a ready market for their work, this period saw one of the most remarkable flourishings of poetic and writing talent in British history, sometimes known as the English Renaissance.

A TIMELINE OF
SHAKESPEARE'S LIFE

A brief chronology of the time during which the Sonnets were probably written. The dates of the plays are approximate.

1564	Apr 23	Shakespeare born in Stratford-upon-Avon.
1573		Henry Wriothesley, Earl of Southampton, born.
1580		William Herbert born.
1583	May 26	Baptism of 'Susanna daughter to William Shakespeare'.
1588		Defeat of the Spanish Armada.
1585–92		'The Lost Years'. Shakespeare possibly working as a lawyer's clerk or possibly at sea during this time.
1590		Earl of Southampton aged 17.
	Mar	*Henry VI* performed at the Rose (company included Ned Alleyn).
	April	Shakespeare aged 26.
	August	Major outbreaks of Plague. Theatres closed until 26 Dec 1593.
1593	printed	*Venus and Adonis* dedicated to Southampton (see page 160).
	Sept 17	*The Unfortunate Traveller*, Nashe. Dedicated to Southampton.
	Sept 30	Marlowe murdered 'in Tavern brawl at Deptford'.
1594	publ	*Titus Andronicus, Two Gentlemen of Verona, Taming of the Shrew*.
	publ	*The Rape of Lucrece*, dedicated to Southampton (see page 160)
	publ	*Shadow of Night*, George Chapman.
	publ	*The Terror of the Night*, Thomas Nashe.
	Oct	The Theatre opens at Shoreditch with The Lord Chamberlain's Men.
1595	acted	*Romeo and Juliet, Richard II*.
		Apprentice Riots. Theatres closed again.
1596	acted	*Merchant of Venice, Henry IV pt I*.
	publ	*Richard II*.
		Essex led the Azores Expedition.

Raleigh imprisoned for secret marriage to Elizabeth Throckmorton, a Maid of Honour to the Queen.

1597 May 4   Shakespeare buys 'New Place', second-largest property in Stratford.

Sept   Shakespeare in cast of Jonson's *Every Man in his Humour*. William Herbert comes to London aged 17.

Southampton marries Mistress Vernon, Lady-in-Waiting to Queen Elizabeth, and is imprisoned for it.

1598 acted   *Henry IV pt II, Much Ado About Nothing*.

publ   *Love's Labour's Lost, Richard III*.

publ   *The Passionate Pilgrim*, an anthology, printed by William Jaggard, containing versions of Sonnets 138 and 144, and extracts from *Love's Labours Lost*, yet claiming on the title page that the rest of the book was by Shakespeare.

1599 acted   *Henry V, Julius Caesar, As You Like It* (?)

publ   *Romeo and Juliet*

The Globe Theatre built on the South Bank from the timbers of Burbage's The Theatre. Shakespeare mentioned as a sharer (partner) and actor in The Lord Chamberlain's Men.

Essex's disastrous expedition to Ireland. Southampton made General of Horse, but removed again by Elizabeth's express command. Essex put under virtual house arrest on his return. Southampton seen frequently in playhouse.

1600 acted ?   *Hamlet, Twelfth Night, The Merry Wives of Windsor*.

printed   *Much Ado About Nothing, A Midsummer Night's Dream, Henry IV pt II, Henry V*.

Shakespeare aged 36. Elizabeth ill.

1601   Herbert succeeds his father as Earl of Pembroke, aged 21. Mary Fitton bears a child to Herbert, who refuses to marry her and is briefly imprisoned by the Queen.

Feb 8   Essex Rebellion thwarted. Essex (aged 34) and all leaders executed except Southampton, who was imprisoned in the Tower. It would appear he co-operated and bought his life.

1602 printed   *The Merry Wives of Windsor, Troilus and Cressida*.

1603	printed	*Hamlet*.
		Elizabeth I dies. James VI of Scotland becomes King.
1604		Herbert (aged 24) marries. (Shakespeare 40; Southampton 31.)
1609	printed	*Sonnets* publ. by Thomas Thorpe, with *A Lover's Complaint*.
1612		Only recorded reference made to *Sonnets* before 1640.
1616		Shakespeare dies at Statford, aged 52.
1623	printed	First Folio containing all extant plays, except *Pericles*, put together by Hemmings and Condell, dedicated to William and Philip Herbert.
1640	printed	*Sonnets* published for the first time after 1609, by Benson.

CRITICAL APPROACHES

Shakespeare's Sonnets can be studied from a variety of critical perspectives. The Sonnets raise many questions such as: 'How do they relate to Shakespeare's own experience?', 'Can we read them chronologically as a personal story or was their order imposed later by Shakespeare or someone other than Shakespeare?' and 'Who were the Friend, the Rival Poet and the Woman (often referred to as 'The Dark Lady')?

Such questions have led some critics to approach the Sonnets like a detective hunt, attempting to identify people and events. A historical approach (looking at the Sonnets through their possible references to contemporary events and people) can be useful, as background knowledge can help us to understand more about the poems themselves. The biographical approach (tracing the poet's relationship with the Friend and the Woman) is also valid up to a point. However, we must be careful not to assume the poetic 'I' of the Sonnets and Shakespeare are one, that the emotions expressed in the Sonnets are always Shakespeare's own. That is not to say we should read the Sonnets as entirely fictional either: it is likely that in some sonnets Shakespeare identified with the poet while in others the poet's is a rhetorical or dramatic voice.

The Sonnets can also be approached through explorations of their style, form, images and themes. Many of the sonnets are fascinating in their own right because of their individual use of the sonnet form, powerful imagery, ambiguous and shifting meanings and expressions of emotion and thought. *Shakespeare's Sonnets* can also be approached as one coherent poem through the many links and echoes between sonnets. While it may be debatable that the Sonnets form a psychological narrative, it is still possible to read them as a whole through their many patterns of imagery, themes and emotions.

You will find all of these approaches useful in helping you to explore and enjoy the Sonnets. They are outlined in detail in separate sections below. The Timeline (on pages 156–8) is a quick reference to Shakespeare's life and the characters and events surrounding the production of the Sonnets.

Remember that you bring your own knowledge of language, cultural background and ideas to the Sonnets – and that four hundred years of changes in culture and language have passed since they were written.

You must be aware of the range of meanings or connotations words carry. Within the interpretation of a word or an image, you will often find other significant and half-intended implications and ideas.

Ordering the Sonnets and the biographical approach

This edition adopts the order of the Sonnets to be found in the 1609 Quarto published by Thomas Thorpe.

Shakespeare probably wrote most of his sonnets during the 1590s when sonnet sequences were extremely fashionable (see **The sonnet form**, page 162) but the sequence does not appear to have been printed during that time. In 1598, a minor poet, Francis Meres, mentioned Shakespeare's 'sugared sonnets among his private friends', so it is probable that the Sonnets were circulated amongst a select group of people in the 1590s but not published. Literature was often circulated in manuscript form and then published at a later date – not always with the permission of the author!

Thomas Thorpe probably published the Sonnets for his own gain and possibly with malicious intent. It is widely believed that Shakespeare worked with the printer on earlier poems (***Venus and Adonis*** and ***The Rape of Lucrece*** of 1593–4) and these poems carry a dedication over Shakespeare's name to the Earl of Southampton. However, in 1609, the Sonnets were published with a dedication by Thomas Thorpe, not by Shakespeare. It is possible, therefore, that the Sonnets were published without Shakespeare's involvement. It is possible that Shakespeare did not want the Sonnets to be published, perhaps because they were partly autobiographical and too personal.

Whether or not Shakespeare was involved in the publication and ordering of the 1609 Sonnets, it is unlikely that they were written in the order they appear. The order is quite neat and probably not accidental: all the poems addressed to the young man (or 'Friend') appear in the first 126 sonnets while all those concerning a woman are among the remaining 28. Over the years various critics have attempted to reorder the sonnets but no one has produced an order which is indisputably better. As you work through this edition you will find that many of the sonnets in the Quarto sequence do follow each other logically (some are linked with an initial 'But' or 'Thus'), the repeated themes in some short sequences make them inseparable (eg, 27–28, 44–45, 57–58) and the first 126 sonnets do appear to tell us of a developing and changing relationship between the poet and the Friend.

The important thing to remember is that while the Sonnets do tell us the story of the poet's involvement with the Friend and the Woman the 'poet's' voice is not necessarily Shakespeare's own. Many of the sonnets do appear to be intensely personal poetry and some may well be autobiographical. Some may be rhetorical speeches (like a speech Shakespeare would write for one of his characters in a play). As you read through this edition it is up to you to decide where you think Shakespeare might be identifying himself with the poetic voice.

The historical approach

Shakespeare is thought to have written his sonnets sometime between 1592 and 1605. 'Shakespeare's sugar'd sonnets' were mentioned in print in 1598, two were printed in 1599, and the whole collection published in 1609, then again in 164, twenty-four years after the poet's death. Exactly why they were written, and who they were addressed to – or written for – remains a mystery to this day, though many have tried to solve it. Shakespeare's plays – 37 (at least) printed between 1592 and 1613 – show distinct similarity with some of the sonnets, especially *Love's Labours Lost* (1593); *Romeo and Juliet* (1595); *Richard II* (1596); *Hamlet* (1601). *Richard III* (1593) contains, word for word, line 14 of Sonnet 94. This helps prove the sonnets to be the work of William Shakespeare and perhaps helps us guess when certain sonnets were written.

There have been many attempts to identify the young man (or Friend) of the sonnet sequence. Some have suggested he is Henry Wriothesley, Earl of Southampton, to whom Shakespeare's narrative poems are dedicated. Others suggest he is William Herbert, Earl of Pembroke, one of the dedicatees of the First Folio. Or perhaps he is a boy actor called William Hughes, as Oscar Wilde supposed in his story, *The Portrait of Mr W H*. The Dark Lady has proved even more elusive and the Rival Poet also remains a great mystery. The fashionable sonneteers of the 1590s whom Shakespeare parodies in Sonnet 30 are unlikely to have been viewed by Shakespeare as great rivals. He may have viewed dramatists and poets Christopher Marlowe or Ben Johnson as rivals or perhaps Thomas Nashe.

While 'solving' the identity of these people would cast some light on some of the poems, we do not need to know their identity to enjoy the Sonnets fully.

The sonnet form

A sonnet is traditionally a single-stanza poem consisting of 14 lines with rhymes arranged in definite schemes. The sonnet was first introduced in England in 1527 when the poet, Sir Thomas Wyatt brought back from Italy some poems by Petrarch. These were called *sonnetto* – little songs of love – to a lady called Laura. Sir Thomas Wyatt began to write his own imitations of these 14-line verses – and the English sonnet was born.

By the end of the sixteenth century the sonnet form had become very popular and the 1590s saw a vogue for sonnet sequences including Sir Philip Sidney's *Astrophel and Stella* (published in 1591), Samuel Daniel's *Sonnets to Delia* (published in 1592), Spencer's *Amoretti* (published in 1595) and Drayton's *Idea's Mirror* (published in 1595). Most were sequences of poems addressed to a young woman. Often, the young woman is beautiful, but inaccessible by reason of her beauty, wealth or high birth, and the poet is desperately in love with her from afar.

The Elizabethan Sonnet Form

Technical terms which are useful in discussing sonnets are:

couplet: a unit of two lines
quatrain: a unit of four lines
sestet: a unit of six lines
octave: a unit of eight lines

These terms are used to describe Sonnet 1 below:

From fairest creatures we desire increase,	a	first quatrain
That thereby beauty's rose might never die,	b	
But as the riper should by time decease,	a	
His tender heir might bear his memory;	b	
But thou, contracted to thine own bright eyes,	c	second quatrain
Feed'st thy light's flame, with self-substantial fuel,	d	
Making a famine where abundance lies,	c	
Thyself thy foe, to thy sweet self too cruel.	d	
Thou that art now the world's fresh ornament	e	third quatrain
And only herald to the gaudy spring	f	
Within thine own bud buriest thy content	e	
And, tender churl, mak'st waste in niggarding.	f	
Pity the world, or else this glutton be:	g	couplet
To eat the world's due, by the grave and thee	g	

You will see that these units are defined by the rhyme schemes within them. For example, in the first quatrain the first and third lines rhyme (a,a) and the second and fourth lines rhyme (b,b). This pattern is known as the Elizabethan sonnet and is the form used by Shakespeare in almost all of his Sonnets.

Shakespeare used the form to express subtle shades of meaning and subverted the conventions of the fashionable sonnet sequence. The notes and activities opposite the poems in this edition, and the activities below, will help you to explore Shakespeare's imaginative use of form and convention.

Approaches through themes and ideas

Shakespeare's Sonnets contain a wonderful range of insights into huge and complex questions such as: What is the nature of love? What is life when threatened with the ravages of time (and ultimately death)? What is the relationship between art and life? His Sonnets are not an attempt to outline a coherent philosophy or consistent train of thought. Rather, they offer snapshots of the poet's preoccupations at the time of writing each sonnet. Through the intensely personal experiences of the poet's relationship with the Friend, the Woman, rival poets, and his fear of time and mortality, they read almost as a spontaneous exploration of the complexities of human life. Exploring the Sonnets through themes and ideas gives us a way of linking the sonnets and viewing them as a whole.

Love

More than anything else, *Shakespeare's Sonnets* are about love. The Sonnets explore the nature of two very different kinds of love: the poet's love for the friend, which seems to be of an idealizing, almost unrealized nature and the poet's more sensual, erotic love for a woman, which he appears to find degrading. Through the poet's changing relationships with these characters the Sonnets explore the nature of love itself. The poet compares the two relationships in Sonnet 144: however, other tormented Sonnets do not suggest his relationship with the Friend was as angelic as 144 suggests.

The poet's relationship with the Friend unfolds more or less sequentially through Sonnets 1–126. Sonnets 127 to 154 are mostly concerned with the poet's relationship with Woman.

You will find activities exploring the theme of **love** in the sonnets on page 170.

Time

Throughout the Sonnets the poet is disturbed by the onward march of time which is taking him ultimately towards death. Time destroys beauty and ultimately, time destroys life. In many Sonnets the poet attempts to overcome the destructive nature of time. In Sonnets 1 to 17 he exhorts the young man to reproduce in order to perpetuate his beauty. In various Sonnets such as 55, 63 and 60 he declares that time will be overcome through his poetry because the Friend will survive in verse. In others, such as 64 and 126, he sounds a far less positive note and submits to the inevitability of time passing.

You will find activities exploring the theme of **time** on page 169.

Life, Nature and Art

Through writing about his relationship with the Friend and the Woman, the poet makes many observations about the relationship between life, nature and art, in this case often about the poet's verse. In Sonnets 78, 79, 82 and 84 it appears the Friend is now the subject of a rival poet and this gives rise to some reflections about the poet's work: to what extent the poet's verse represents the true nature of the subject and to what extent other poets' verse falsifies by adding embellishments. The poet also explores the power of poetry to endure and so defeat time. (See **Time** opposite.)

A linked theme is Shakespeare's exploration of the relationship between outward appearance and inner truth or reality.

Approaches through image patterns

Although *Shakespeare's Sonnets* were probably not written in a coherent order and although each sonnet is a distinct poem in itself, the Sonnets also read like a whole poem because words, phrases and images are repeated and echoed within them. Many repeated images mirror repeated themes: others help us to make more oblique links with other sonnets, giving added layers of meaning to the Sonnet we are reading.

Images of flowers abound throughout the Sonnets. The rose was a conventional image of Elizabethan (and earlier) poetry, traditionally associated with love. Shakespeare does much more than use this image in a conventional way: flower imagery in the Sonnets (rose, bud, flowers, weeds) is linked with the inexorable passing of time and with the Friend's moral and spritual character. (See Sonnets 1, 5, 35, 54, 69, 109.)

Images of the seasons, weather and nature are also linked with the passing of time. (See Sonnets 5, 6, 18 and 104.) Most famous is Sonnet 18 which uses a summer's day as an image for how short-lived youth and love can be. In Sonnets 33 to 35 the change from sunshine to cloud matches a change in the poet's mood. The sun is linked to the Friend's beauty, notably in Sonnets 7, 33 and 73.

There are also many allusions to law (Sonnets 30, 46, 87) about which Shakespeare seems to have had remarkable knowledge; images drawn from classical literature, from music (Sonnets 8, 48), art (Sonnets 16, 21, 24), and the spirit world (Sonnets 80, 86) amongst others.

As you trace imagery through the sonnets remember to look at *how* Shakespeare is using the images to explore emotions and ideas.

ACTIVITIES

The activities in this section are designed to explore in detail specific aspects of individual Sonnets or groups of Sonnets. They should be seen as a springboard for discussion, research, evaluation, personal response and writing. Most can be done either individually or as group work.

The notes you make during these activities will help in planning and writing longer essays.

Looking at single Sonnets

You will find you almost always want to write about a group of Sonnets or about the whole sequence. However, you will always find it invaluable to have explored some sonnets in great detail. If you know some Sonnets very well it is easier to pick up the echoes and repeating patterns in other Sonnets.

The activities below are two different approaches to exploring Sonnets in detail. You will find both of these approaches helpful when you are reading Sonnets closely.

Sonnet 55

1) Read the Sonnet a few times. If possible read it aloud to a partner, then ask your partner to read it to you. Compare your readings. Do you each adopt a different tone? Do you emphasize the same words and phrases?

2) Now explore the Sonnet closely:

a) What is the effect of the negatives in line 1? What is the effect of repeating this structure in line 7?

b) Underline all the **alliteration** (see page 179) in this Sonnet. What is the effect of linking the words 'unswept,' 'stone', 'statues' and 'sluttish' through alliteration?

c) Now look at the rhyme, internal rhyme and **assonance** (see page 179) in this Sonnet. How does the rhyme emphasize the content? (For example, the rhyme of 'rhyme' with 'time' helps to emphasize the triumph of verse over the ravages of time.)

d) Many editors of *Shakespeare's Sonnets* do not follow the punctuation in the Quarto, and the punctuation in the Quarto was probably not

Shakespeare's own. However, it is interesting to look at the way the commas and **enjambment** (see page 179) alter the pace of the poem. Which phrases are emphasized by pauses in the middle of the line?

e) Which lines do you think are the most powerful in emphasizing the argument that the Poet's subject will triumph over time through verse?

3) Write a paragraph about Shakespeare's use of *form* to mirror his *theme* in Sonnet 55.

Sonnet 94

1) Read the Sonnet a few times. If possible read your Sonnet to a partner and ask your partner to read the Sonnet to you. Compare your readings.

2) Read through the Sonnet closely, thinking carefully about the meaning of each line and about how language, imagery and form mirror the meaning:

a) In lines 1 to 4 what is the poet saying about people such as the Friend? How do the rhymes and pace mirror the content?

b) Why do you think the Poet says such people inherit heaven's grace 'Rightly'? Are these lines ironic?

c) What does 'husband nature's riches from expense' mean?

d) Does line 7 refer only to outward appearance or does it also refer to qualities of character? (Think about the rhyme with 'graces'.)

e) What are the two interpretations of line 8?

f) Discuss how line 12 might refer to both the subject's rank and his moral state.

g) What warning is the poet giving to the Friend in the sestet? Does the final couplet alter your reading of the first part of the poem?

Sonnet 130

In this Sonnet Shakespeare uses and subverts the conventions of Elizabethan love poetry. Identify the conventions and think about the way Shakespeare is using them.

Many critics read this poem as a parody of contemporary love poetry and it certainly has a mocking tone. Some critics suggest that Shakespeare is satirizing the conventions in order to mock the Woman. Other critics suggest he is not undermining the Woman, but that he is using conventional images to show that she far surpasses all such images.

Look at the poem closely. Can you make a case for this second interpretation?

Shorter questions on individual Sonnets

Sonnet 1

- Identify the phrases in this Sonnet which suggest that vanity and self-centredness are not necessarily a positive way to live.

- In lines 13–14, the poet makes reference to the canker worm image and accuses the Young Man of devouring his own potential and the potential of another life.

Why does the poet imply that the Young Man is acting beyond his rights in making this decision?

How would you receive this advice?

Sonnet 2

- This Sonnet relies on a **metaphor** (see page 181) drawn from the seasons and their effect on the land, which begins in the first quatrain and is taken up in the final couplet. Starting from why the poet substitutes 'Winters' for 'years', explain the intended message for the subject.

Sonnet 12

- Is the solace offered against the 'wastes of time' convincing? Give reasons for your answer.

Sonnet 14

- Identify the various contrary views of predicting the future Shakespeare includes in this Sonnet. Which of these does he reject – and why?

Sonnet 18

- Find the five beats or strong syllables in each line of the Sonnet. Now read Sonnet 18 to a partner, stressing the **iambic pentameter** (see page 180) you have found.

Discuss why your reading sounded effective or, if not, discuss what you need to do to improve the reading.

Sonnet 80

- Why does the poet not balance line 6 properly, by calling his sail 'humblest' to agree with 'proudest'?
- What evidence is there in this Sonnet that Shakespeare takes this rival very seriously?

Sonnet 128

- How does the poet develop the **extended metaphor** (see page 181) of music in this Sonnet?

Sonnet 138

- How does this Sonnet develop the theme of truth and falsehood?

Sonnet 143

- What is so unusual about the imagery and tone of this Sonnet?

Sonnet 148

- Is the final couplet a **conceit** (see page 179)?

Sonnet 151

- Explain whether the bawdiness of this Sonnet is in its tone or in its imagery.
- How, in the final couplet, can the poet justify his love for the Woman in the face of his conscience?

Patterns of ideas and images

Time

Re-read Sonnets 12, 55, 60, 63, 64, 73, 76, 77, 116 and 126.

All these Sonnets are concerned with the passing of time. In which Sonnets does the poet accept the passing of time as inevitable? In which does he suggest time may be defeated if he or his subject survive in verse?

a) Look carefully at how time is portrayed in each Sonnet. How do the imagery, use of poetic devices such as **alliteration** (see page 179), and pace affect the tone of each Sonnet? Which Sonnets ring with confidence? Which are sad and dejected? Which offer tentative hope?

b) Look at Sonnet 76. Do you think the poet finds solace in the fact he always writes of the same subject in the same form? Why?

c) In Sonnet 55 the poet asserts that poetry will triumph over the ravages of time. In Sonnet 116 he suggest that love defeats time because it is constant and absolute. Which Sonnet do you find most convincing? Justify your answer with reference to the imagery, pace and tone of each Sonnet.

Love

a) In Sonnet 144 the poet writes of his two loves 'of comfort and despair', referring to his love for the Young Man and his love for the Woman. How does the balanced form of this poem reflect its content?

b) Trace the development of the poet's relationship with the Young Man throughout the first 126 Sonnets. In which Sonnets does the poet love the young man with a pure, idealizing love? In which poems does the poet forgive the young man for minor discrepancies? In which poems is the poet tortured because the Young Man has turned away from him? In which does he forgive the Young Man?

What evidence is there that the poet's relationship with the Young Man was not the always the 'comfort' which Sonnet 144 suggests?

c) In Sonnet 116 the poet describes an ideal love as a meeting of minds. In Sonnet 129 he describes a carnal love which disturbs him. Compare the imagery and pace of the two poems.

d) Read Sonnets 129, 132, 137 and 138. How would you summarize the poet's relationship with the Woman? (Use evidence from the poems in your answer.)

The Natural World

a) Trace images of flowers, weeds, buds and roses throughout the Sonnets. (Keep notes of references.) Are the images used to reflect similar themes in different Sonnets? How does the use of the images change throughout the sequence?

b) Now do the same for images of the seasons.

Comparing Sonnets

Sonnets 1–17

■ Shakespeare is concerned to pick up the Young Man's vanity in several of the 17 poems. Choose a small selection of these references and discuss whether you think the older man's advice is consistent on this point.

Sonnets 2 and 3

■ With a partner, copy the first quatrain (see page 163) of Sonnet 2 while your partner copies the first quatrain of Sonnet 3. Now mark/above each strong syllable or beat. Compare your result with your partner's. One poem should have masculine endings, one should have feminine endings. Which is which?

Sonnets 29 and 30

■ These two Sonnets have a similar theme and use similar imagery, yet their structure is different. One is an octet and a sestet while the other is three quatrains and a couplet. Identify the similar themes and imagery, and which has which structure. Then explain which poem you prefer and why.

Sonnets 40–42

■ Do you think these three poems were written as a set? Find as much evidence as you can in the theme and the language of the Sonnets to justify your view.

Sonnets 56 and 60

Which of these two Sonnets uses the image of the sea most effectively?

Sonnets 71–73

■ Is it possible to find any contrast in the tone of these two poems? Does the tone convey the poet's meaning effectively in either Sonnet? Explain your answer by referring to imagery as well as tone.

Sonnets 97–98

These two Sonnets share a theme but treat it using different imagery. What is the theme and which treatment do you prefer? Explain your answer with close reference to the texts, contrasting as many images from the two Sonnets as you can.

ESSAY QUESTIONS

1) Although Shakespeare only uses one form of verse, does he manage to explore its full potential?

2) 'The Sonnets of Shakespeare prove love poetry to be timeless.' How far do you agree with this premise?

3) 'A complex love-story, rich in character and incident.' How far do you agree with this view of *Shakespeare's Sonnets?*

4) Discuss whether the Sonnets are best interpreted as one story or many separate poems.

5) Choosing one Sonnet addressed to the Friend, and one to the Dark Lady, discuss the differences between their tone, imagery and themes.

6) Choose three poems and analyse the development of imagery to convey Shakespeare's meaning.

7) Compare the imagery of Sonnet 8 with that of Sonnet 128.

8) In the Sonnets how does the imagery connected with disease and decay emphasize Shakespeare's view of death?

9) How far do you agree that in the Sonnets Shakespeare is more concerned with the pain and heartache of relationships than with their success?

10) 'In reading *Shakespeare's Sonnets,* we experience the whole range of human emotion.' Explain how three different Sonnets have moved you in different ways.

11) 'The relationships in the Sonnets are profound rather than trivial.' How far do you agree with this statement?

12) 'Shakespeare is less enamoured of the Dark Lady than he is of his Friend.' Discuss.

13) Is the poet of *Shakespeare's Sonnets* a lonely figure?

14) How far is the theme of the war against time a preoccupation in the Sonnets?

15) With close reference to three of *Shakespeare's Sonnets,* discuss how the poet honours beauty.

16) To what extent to you think Shakespeare was terrified by the passing of time?

17) Discuss Shakespeare's presentation of friendship in the Sonnets.

18) Choose three Sonnets which have made a particularly strong impression on you and explain how they have achieved this impression.

WRITING AN ESSAY
ABOUT POETRY

You own personal response to a poet and his or her work is of major importance when writing an essay on poetry, either as part of your course or as an examination question. However, this personal response needs to be based on a solid concept of how poetry works, so you must clearly show that you understand the methods the poet uses to convey the message and ideas of the poem to the reader. In most cases, unless it is relevant to your answer, you should not pad out your essay with biographical or background material.

Planning

Look carefully at the wording of the question. Underline the important words and ideas. Make sure you apply your mind to these key elements of the question and then explore them in the essay.

Bring all your knowledge of, and opinions on, a poet and his or her poetry to this first stage of writing. Brainstorm your ideas and always combine these thoughts in a plan that shows the development and intention of your answer. Your plan must outline the structure of your essay. In exam conditions, the plan and the direction of your comments may take you only a few minutes and should be little more than a way of laying out your ideas in order. However the plan must be an outline of how and where you are going to link your evidence to the opinions and concepts of the essay. Reject any ideas which are not relevant at the planning stage. Remember that your plan should be arranged around your ideas and not the chronological order of a poem or a poet's work, or your essay will be weakened.

Writing

Your introduction must implicitly or, if you wish, explicitly make the teacher or examiner realize that you understand the question.

Don't spent a lot of time spotting, defining and examining poetic techniques and form. If you do identify these features, then you must be sure of the poetic terms and be able to show why they are significant in the verse and to the poet's attempts to create a 'meaning' and a message. The Glossary of Literary Terms might help you.

Make absolutely sure that your answer is clear and that it tackles the issues in the question precisely. Try to offer points for discussion and apply your knowledge in an interesting way. Don't go ahead and disregard what the question asks you to write about, then write the essay you want to write. Don't waffle, don't write too elaborately or use terms vaguely; at the same time, don't be too heavy-handed with your views. Strive to put your opinions directly and accurately.

In exam conditions be aware of the time, and if you are running out of your allotted span then make sure that you put down your most important ideas in the minutes left. Try to leave a few minutes to revise and proof-read your script. Be sure that the points you have made make sense and are well supported by evidence. Don't try to introduce new ideas as you write unless they are essential to your essay. Often these extra thoughts can distract you from the logic of your argument. If it is essential, then refer back to your plan and slot the idea into the right part of the essay.

Bring your ideas together at the end of the essay. Make sure that you have put your views clearly and, if necessary, express the main thrust of your views or argument again.

Quotations

Quotations are a vital source of evidence for the viewpoints and ideas you express in your essay. Try not to misquote and remember that when using extracts of more than a few words you should place them separately outside your text as they would be laid out in the poem.

If you follow the advice here you will produce a clear, relevant and logical essay. Try to spend time reading and listening to the comments of your teacher and make your own notes on your work for revision purposes.

Andrew Whittle

A NOTE FROM A CHIEF EXAMINER

Your examination script is the medium through which you communicate with your examiner. As a student, you will have studied what writers say and how they say it; your examiner will assess what *you* say and how you say it. This is the simple process through which your knowledge and understanding of the texts you have studied is converted into your examination result.

The questions which you will find on your examination paper have been designed to enable you to display your ability to engage in short, highly concentrated explorations of particular aspects of the texts which you have studied. There is no intention to trick you into making mistakes, rather to enable you to demonstrate to your examiner your knowledge and understanding. Questions take a variety of forms. For a poetry text, you may be asked to concentrate on one poem, or a particular group of them, and provide detailed examination of some features of the writing. You may be asked to range widely throughout a poet's work, exploring specified aspects of his of her style and themes. You may be asked to provide a considered personal reaction to a critical evaluation of the poet's work.

Whatever the question, you are, ultimately, being asked to explore what and how, content and style. Equally, you are being asked for a personal response. You are communicating to your examiner your own understanding of the text, and your reactions to it, based on the studies you have undertaken.

All of this may seem very simple, if not self-evident, but it is worthwhile to devote some time to thinking about what an examination is, and how it works. By doing so, you will understand why it is so important that you should prepare yourself for your examination in two principal ways: first, by thorough, thoughtful and analytical textual study, making your own well-informed evaluation of the work of a particular writer, considering what he or she is conveying to you, how this is done, how you react, and what has made you respond in that way; then, by practising the writing skills which you will need to convey all these things to your examiner.

When assessing your script and awarding marks, examiners are working to guidelines which instruct them to look for a variety of different qualities in an essay.

These are some of the things which an examiner will consider.

- How well has the candidate understood the essay question and the given task? Is the argument, and the material used to support it, entirely relevant?
- Is quotation used aptly, and textual reference employed skillfully in discussion?
- Is the candidate aware of how and why the writer has crafted material in a particular way?
- Is there evidence of engagement with the text, close analytical reading, and awareness of subtleties in interpretation?
- Does the candidate have the necessary vocabulary, both general and critical, to express his or her understanding lucidly? Are technical terms integrated into discussion?
- Can the candidate provide an interesting, clearly expressed and structured line of argument, which fully displays a well-informed personal response?

From these points, you should be able to see the kind of approach to examination questions which you should avoid. Re-hashed notes, second-hand opinion, unsupported assertion and arid copies of marginal jottings have no place in a good script. Don't fall into the trap of reproducing a pre-planned essay. Undoubtedly you will find (if your preparation has been thorough) that you are drawing on ideas which you have already explored in other essays, but all material used must be properly adapted to the task you are given. Don't take a narrative approach; paraphrase cannot replace analysis. Do not, under any circumstances, copy out chunks of introduction or critical notes from your text in an open book examination. Nor do you need to quote at excessive length; your examiner knows the text.

It is inevitable that, when writing in examination conditions, you will only use quite a small amount of the material you have studied in order to answer a particular question. Don't feel that what you are not using has been wasted. It hasn't. All your studies will have informed the understanding you display in a succinct, well-focused answer, and will equip you to write a good essay.

Virginia Graham
Chief Examiner for A-level Literature

S E L E C T
B I B L I O G R A P H Y

Editions

The Sonnets William Shakespeare ed. M.R. Ridley: Dent, Everyman. 1934

Shakespeare's Sonnets edited by Stanley Wells: Oxford. 1985

The Sonnets and A Lover's Complaint by William Shakespeare ed John Kerrigan: New Penguin Shakespeare. 1986

The Sonnets and Narrative Poems Introduction to the Sonnets by W.H. Auden: Signet. 1964

Shakespeare's Sonnets ed. Stephen Booth: Yale. 1977

New Poems by Shakespeare; Order and Meaning restored to the Sonnets John Padel: Herbert. 1981

Shakespeare's Sonnets. S.C. Campbell: Bell & Hyman. 1978

Shakespeare's Sonnets ed. W.G. Ingram and Theodore Redpath: Hodder and Stoughton. 1964, 1978

Detectives

Only Begotten Sonnets S.C. Campbell. Bell & Hyman. 1978

The Secrets of Shakespeare's Sonnets Roderick L. Eagle. Mitre. 1965

Biography

Shakespeare Anthony Burgess, Jonathan Cape. 1970; Penguin. 1972.

GLOSSARY OF LITERARY TERMS

alliteration Also known as head-rhyme – the repetition for effect of the initial consonants or vowels of words in a sequence. Sonnet 55 is notably alliterative:

> Not *m*arble *n*or the gilded *m*onuments
> Of *p*rinces shall outlive this *p*owerful rhyme
> But you *sh*all *sh*ine more bright in these contents
> Than un*s*wept *s*tone be*s*meared with *s*luttish time …

allusion An indirect reference. Whereas direct quotations usually have acknowledged sources the allusion usually has no acknowledged source. It is often cryptic so the audience has to make the connection to the orginial source.

assonance A form of rhyme in which the vowel sounds correspond but the consonants do not, or *vice versa*, e.g. *late/take, make/mark*. Assonance can be used either internally, i.e. within the line, or at the ends of lines in place of full rhymes.

conceit A poetic conceit is a far-fetched, audaciously ingenious extended comparison which is often carried through a complete verse, several verses or indeed throughout the whole poem. It was employed to outstanding effect by the Metaphysical Poets, principally John Donne.

end-stopping An end-stopped line is one where the sense is a self-contained unit which finishes at the end of the line and is marked by a short pause or break at that point. See Sonnet 90:

> Then hate me when thou wilt, if ever, now,
> Now while the world is bent my deeds to cross,
> Join with the spite of fortune, make me bow,
> And do not drop in for an after-loss.

enjambment This is the term used to describe the continuation of the sense of a line of verse beyond the end of that line without a pause. See Sonnet 63, where the first two lines are end-stopped and lines 3-5 enjambed:

Against my love shall be as I am now,
With time's injurious hand crushed and o'erworn,
When hours have drain'd his blood and filled his brow
With lines and wrinkles; when his youthful morn
Hath travelled on to age's steepy night...

half-rhyme   This is a rhyme which is approximate only. Sonnet 1 contains an example of half-rhyme in the first quatrain, where line 2 ends with *die* and the line 4 with *memory*. It is impossible always to be certain whether such approximate rhymes were part of the poet's repertoire of techniques or whether they represent a change in pronunciation or stress which has occurred over the centuries.

hexameter   A line of six metrical feet. (See **iambic pentameter** below).

iambic pentameter   The iambic pentameter is the meter (or rhythmic pattern) of the Shakespearean Sonnet. An iamb is a foot, or metrical unit, of two syllables – a weak (unstressed) syllable followed by a strong (stressed) one. Words such as *convey*, *repent* are iambs. The iambic pentameter is a line containing five iambic feet as in Sonnet 22.

My glass shall not persuade me I am old,
So long as youth and thou are of one date

irony   A rhetorical device, employed for deliberate effect, for conveying meaning through words whose literal meaning is completely the opposite. Mark Antony's funeral oration over Caesar (*Julius Caesar* III.2) is an extended exercise in irony:

They that have done this deed are honourable.
What private griefs they have, alas, I know not,
That made them do it; they are wise and honourable,
And will no doubt with reasons answer you.
I come not, friends, to steal away your hearts;
I am no orator, as Brutus is,
But, as you know me all, a plain, blunt man
That love my friend...

Shakespeare appears to be using irony when he praises the work of the Rival Poet and depreciates his own lack of learning and inferior verse, when we know from other sonnets in the sequence that he was well aware of the worth of his own 'powerful rhyme' (Sonnet 55).

metaphor An implicit comparison in which something is referred to as *being* the thing which it resembles as in Sonnet 3:

> Thou art thy mother's glass, and she in thee
> Calls back the lovely April of her prime;

Most complex is the extended metaphor in which several different facets of the comparison are linked to several corresponding facets of the thing it resembles. For example, the way the season of winter resembles the poet's old age in Sonnet 73.

Aptly employed, metaphor is a much more powerful and immediate figure of speech than **simile** (see page 182), which is an explicit comparison of one thing with another, e.g.

> My love is like a red, red rose

or, as in Sonnet 60:

> Like as the waves make towards the pebbled shore,
> So do our minutes hasten to their end...

oxymoron A figure of speech which joins opposed or contradictory terms in a single phrase, e.g.

> darkly bright (Sonnet 43)

paradox A self-contradictory statement, e.g.

> And brass eternal slave to mortal rage (Sonnet 64)

or

> When most I wink, then do my eyes best see (Sonnet 43)

pastoral A literary genre which purported to describe (albeit in an idealised and unrealistic manner) the lives of shepherds and rustics, and which enjoyed a resurgence of popularity in the sixteenth century (Spenser '*The Faerie Queene*'; '*The Shephearde's Calendar*'; Sir Philip Sidney '*Astrophel and Stella*'; as well as pastoral episodes in many of Shakespeare's plays, e.g. *As You Like It, The Winter's Tale*). It has tended to recur in the works of authors as diverse as Milton, Gay, Wordsworth and Thomas Hardy up to the twentieth century.

personification As a literary device, personification ascribes personaility or human qualities to abstract concepts like Time, Death, the Seasons etc.

pun A play on words which makes use of similarity between different words or of a word's different meanings. See Shakespeare's play on the different senses of Will and his own name in Sonnet 135.

simile See note under **metaphor** above. Fowler's *Modern English Usage* has an illuminating entry – amounting almost to a short essay – on these devices.

synonym A word that means the same as another.

zeugma A figure of speech in which two different words are 'yoked together' by a third which appears to stand in the same relation to both of them but in fact makes sense with only one, e.g. Sonnet 55:

> Nor Mars his sword, nor war's quick fire shall burn
> The living record of your memory.

'Burn' makes perfect sense with 'war's quick fire' but not with 'Mars his sword', for which another verb must be supplied. The effect of zeugma is sometimes unintentionally comic, e.g.

> See Pan with flocks, with fruits Pomona crowned.

While it is easy enough to visualize a goddess of plenty crowned with fruit, an image of the god of flocks and herds similarly crowned is difficult to contemplate!